The Queen and the Princess

A Guide for Mothers and Daughters-In-Law.

Drop the drama and live happily ever after.

Pamela Reynolds

Copyright © 2017 Pamela Reynolds

All rights reserved.

Published by:
Blooming Twig Books
New York / Tulsa
www.bloomingtwig.com

ISBN-978-1-61343-122-1

DEDICATION

This book is dedicated with love
To my husband Paul J. Reynolds, who
Supported and encouraged me.

Contents

Chapter 1 – Who's in Charge	9
Power Struggle	10
Decisions	12
Step Parents	13
Story 1	15
Discussion 1	16
Story 2	16
Discussion 2	19
Reflections for Mothers-in-Law	21
Questions for Mothers-In-Law	22
Chapter 2 – Triumph and Defeat	23
Story 3	25
Discussion 3	28
Reflections for Mothers-in-Law	29
Questions for Mothers-in-Law	30
Chapter 3 – Holiday Crises	31
Visiting	33
When Daughters-In-Law Visit	34
Story 4	36
Discussion 4	38
Reflections for Mothers-in-Law	39
Questions for Mothers-in-Law	40
Chapter 4 – Money Misery	41
Reflections for Mothers-in-Law	43

Questions for the Mother-in-Law	44
Chapter 5 – Jealousy Is Poisonous	45
Son Praises Wife	46
Narrow Minded Gossip	48
Story 5	49
Discussion 5	50
Reflections for Mothers-in-Law	53
Questions for the Mother-in-Law	54
Chapter 6 – Respect Mistakes	55
Story 6	58
Discussion 6	60
Reflections for Mothers-in-Law	62
Questions for Mothers-in-Law	63
Chapter 7 - Overcome Fear	64
Fluidity of Pride and Status	65
Strength in Challenges	66
Story 7	66
Discussion 7	69
Reflections for Mothers-in-Law	71
Questions for Mothers-in-Law	72
Chapter 8 – Courage to Compromise	73
Story 8	75
Discussion 8	78
Reflections for Mothers-in-Law	79
Questions for Mothers-in-Law	80

Chapter 9 – Tolerate Failures and Changes	81
Story 9	83
Discussion 9	85
Story 10	86
Discussion 10	88
Reflections for Mothers-in-Law	89
Questions for Mothers-in-Law	90
Chapter 10 - Children & Grandchildren	91
Considerations for the Mother-in-Law	92
Disciplining	94
Story 11	95
Discussion 11	96
Story 12	97
Discussion 12	98
Reflections for Mothers-in-Law	100
Questions for Mothers-in-Law	101
Acknowledgements	102

ACKNOWLEDGEMENTS

Dr. Emily Stanford	Helen Haley
Margaret O'Neill	Babette Haley
Jen Bundy	Gina Latino
Doris Shannon	Grace Benoit
Sharon Woodman	Jill Nicholas
Linda Cahill	Gracie Benoit
Teresa Benoit	Marge Collette
Mary Shannon	Phyllis Reynolds
Dolores Ruffo	Suzanne Carlson
Helen Stroiney	Judi Manfre
Lisa Bergman	Carol Chatterton
Carolyn Lagassie	Cathy Levesque
Beth Crotty	Cheryl Spencer
Heather Colapinto	Dina Murray
Doreen Brady	Diane Kuzmeski
Nancy Hindes	Shelley Cutter
Barbara Iovaine	Valerie Stanford

I give thanks to numerous others, over the years, who wished to remain anonymous.

Chapter 1 – Who's in Charge

"There are two ways of exerting one's strength: one is pushing down, the other is pulling up." - Booker T. Washington

Evolving into our own person requires strength of character and confidence in the ability to make decisions. When an acknowledgement of power is understood, responsibility is accepted. Playing fair is not easy, and even grownups hate to take turns. Adults teach kids how to play fair. What children are taught about fairness is what needs to be emulated in daily living. With insight, freedom is developed. When there is reflection, the trauma others experience is felt on a higher level by others.

Control and power are dominant in the mother-in-law, daughter-in-law relationship. Mothers guide and control their children throughout their growing years in order to keep them safe and teach them the norms of society. Handing over power and control to a daughter-in-law who is little more than a stranger is unnerving and difficult to do. The trust has not yet been established. The future daughter-in-law is only known and understood by the fiancée. She is privy to family secrets through her relationship with the son, but she does not have the rooted love and family ties. Her judgements at this moment in time are influenced by facts but not heart and soul.

After the marriage, the husband and wife should make their own decisions without the mother-in-law's interference. Right from the beginning, the mother-in-law must accept the quick rise the daughter-in-law makes to a position of power in the family. This is awkward for the mother-in-law, and she might feel devalued. It is a major life change, and handling it can be uncomfortable. Like any changes in life, there are happy and difficult adjustments. The mother-in-law may still have influence but to a lesser degree.

Authority actually comes from respect. When there is respect, there is no fear of being harmed. If the mother-in-law or daughter-in-law has no fear of the other, they trust any decisions made will not bring any injury. Respect encourages mindfulness, which keeps everyone's ego intact. By acknowledging the opinions and differences each person has and shares, compassion for each other is established.

At the beginning of the relationship, both women must tread slowly and cautiously while adjusting to the alterations of life. The playing field has changed, and time and reflection are the friends of both women. More adjustments are inevitable. A son has moved on to a new beginning, and this necessitates freedom and independence. The mother-in-law wants time to make the necessary adjustments. She must reclaim her individuality and move on with her own life. No one has to lose love, which is a critical component of the frustration and fear.

Mothers-in-law are floating aimlessly, wondering what rights they have to say or do anything without getting into trouble. It does get easier, but a display of consideration from their daughters-in-law makes it easier to settle their fears.

Power Struggle

"When the one great scorer comes to write against your name-he marks- not that you won or lost but how you played the game."
- Grantland Rice.

Unchecked power and control breeds destruction. Authority requires tolerance for others who are influenced by this power. Mothers-in-law have the ability to manipulate their sons. If there is a decision that must be made, they can prompt him to pick the choice they want without the use of force. Freedom is the ability to choose and to be accountable for those choices.

It is difficult and unfair to control others through fear or guilt. The surveys discussions and observations prove that to be true. Either option promotes feelings of distrust. Mothers can be experts at using guilt in order to get any child to do jobs or errands for them. Children always want to please mom, and they endure circumstances with perseverance even when they are adults. Of course there are many mothers who are unaware of the amount of guilt they are dumping on their children.

Adult children continue following a mother's advice unconsciously because they have strong bonds of trust with their mother. This can infuriate the daughter-in-law who wants independence for herself and her husband. Husbands have a commitment to their wives and their own households.

The wife is competing against the mother-in-law and this causes tension and stress. She also worries about disappointing her husband. She is aware of how much this woman is loved by her husband. The daughter-in-law would like to make the woman disappear on the one hand, and on the other hand, she wants to befriend this important woman in her husband's life.

Anticipating problems helps heal the wounds of transforming lives. Although the changes are good, they are still adjustments. The shifts force even the simplest routines of life to change. People are happy with routines. The mother-in-law, daughter-in-law relationship is at an early stage, and both women are fearful of the unknown. They may want to be friends, but they must be aware they have to tread slowly in order to respectfully establish their freedom.

Decisions

"The only freedom which deserves the name is that of pursuing our own good, in our own way, so long as we do not attempt to deprive others of theirs, or impede their efforts to obtain it." - John Stuart Mill

It is important for the mother-in-law to take a step back and allow the couple privacy and space. A mother must consider, and respect that her son has a wife to consider. They are now forming their own household, and their business is personal. Probing into confidential affairs is unthinkable. Privacy should always be considered a priority, and mothers-in-law should not interfere or ask their sons for information. Many mothers-in-law lament that their knowledge is completely ignored.

Unfortunately, they must accept such occurrences and understand with the buildup of confidence, the daughters-in-law might be willing to ask for advice. This lack of trust in the mother-in-law unintentionally hurts many mothers-in-law and sets the grounds for disagreements. The same young man, who always placed his trust in his mother and allowed her to influence his judgment, may infuriate his wife if he requests any input from his mother. The wife may perceive it as disloyalty to her. The mother adds fuel to the fire if she encourages this behavior. The best rule is to offer advice only when asked and only at the time one is asked. The son is committed to his wife. He has a place in his heart for both women, but his life is continuing forward with a new woman by his side. The sooner his mother grasps this, the quicker she will find peace.

When a young man coerces his mother into voicing an opinion and agreeing with him, he has done a grave injustice to both his wife and his mother. This strains the relationship between the two women. If a mother-in-law has trust and faith in her son, it should give her the confidence to let go and let her son live his own life.

Parents and even siblings on both sides can damage relationships by exuding pressure in the form of jealousy and competition. For example, the mother of the bride can exert pressure on the daughter out of her jealousy of the mother-in-law, daughter-in-law relationship. Some mothers have convinced their daughters to refrain from becoming close to this woman.

The mother-in-law's daughter can place pressure on the mother to keep her distance with the daughter-in-law. Sisters-in-law in all combinations can be guilty of jealousy. As much as a young couple may attempt to please both sides of the family, they discover it is not possible to make everything equal or to make everyone happy. Some visit one family for a few hours and enjoy the quiet time. The quality of the time spent with others is more valuable than the quantity. If the couple is less manipulated, they can spend more time simply enjoying the company of family on both sides. Competition of any kind makes people uneasy. Plato stated it succinctly when he said, "People are like dirt. They can both nourish you and help you grow as a person or they can stunt your growth and make you wilt and die."

Step Parents

"Real education should educate us out of self into something far finer; into a selflessness which links us with all humanity." - Nancy Astor

Step parents are the background people that wield a lot of power within the moment and behind the scenes. The step-mother may not be close with the step-son or step-daughter yet she is given a position of importance at a wedding regardless of how upsetting this is to the biological relatives. Biological parents cringe at the idea of finding room for these players. They can be on the have to invite part of the guest list unless they have played a significant role in the child's life the step parents who have been actively engaged in the upbringing are in another category. Most step parents remind even the adult kids of an unhappy time in their lives.

The biological mother can feel undermined and less attractive when the step mother outshines her with the clothes, astuteness, or demeanor. When step-parents stay in the background, they are doing a good deed in downplaying their role and eliminating some jealousy as well as antagonism. It is not their time of honor, nor is the wedding about them. It necessitates their attempt at remaining quiet and maintaining the peace.

Demonstrating they are younger or more beautiful is not necessary. It is the bride and grooms' day. The parents have the stage to show how proud they are of their children. When the atmosphere is spoiled, it makes the wedding day an unhappy memory for the couple. A bride does not want her mother to feel inferior, and a groom does not want his mother feeling belittled. Some mothers confessed during discussions they actually threatened to stay at home and skip the wedding rather than face a person who was part of a hurtful history. For many people, the pain never goes away, and the person's presence is a reminder. Telling someone to ignore it is not an easy thing to do.

Like people in high school who tantalized us and left a scar, the person can do it all over again with just their presence. Some divorces end peacefully or in agreement. Some step parents fill the role as a parent due to a death or desertion by the biological parent. That is an exception. Most divorces usually end in fighting, anger, and frustration. Nobody wants to revisit or be reminded of that period of life.

The step-parent's duty is to refrain from upsetting anyone. If they care at all for the young man or woman, they will proceed cautiously and recognize the rehearsal and wedding is not the place for any verbal disagreements or left over anger and revenge. Biological mothers and fathers need to attend their sons or daughter's wedding with joy regardless of their emotional suffering. The focus is on the bride and groom. It is an act of love if a divorced mother or father can remain calm and loving at their child's wedding. It is a true gift of unconditional love, but it is extremely difficult to do. It epitomizes what Theodore Roosevelt once said, "In a moment of decision the best thing you can do is the right thing. The worst thing you can do is nothing."

Story 1

"Courage is doing what you're afraid to do. There can be no courage unless you're scared."

- Eddie Rickenbacker

I went to a friend's wedding and commiserated with her over the absence of her mother. Her parents were divorced and the mother refused to come because my friend had invited the father and his wife. The mother was devastated and cried constantly.

On the day of the wedding, the father and his wife were seated at a table near the mother's table. The mother had refused to come. The step-mother was dressed extremely elegant with not one extra pound obviously younger than my friend's mother. I felt sad the mother was not attending, but she suddenly appeared. I couldn't believe my eyes, and I honestly thought how brave she was to attend and face her own fears. I admired her at that moment and decided I would not have blamed her if she chose to stay home and avoid the confrontation.

I found myself observing the step-mother and noticed her severe straight pose and unsmiling face. She was polite but like a piece of glass. Her dress was more extravagant than the bride's mother's dress.

The mother who was a little overweight, but she was also

stunning. Her face was lit up as she looked at her daughter, and she spoke with the many guests. Her dress was subdued but beautiful. Her smile and manner outmatched any other person who was attending. Her beauty and radiance could not be hidden.

Discussion 1

"In the depths of winter I finally learned that there was in me an invincible summer." - Albert Camus

The mother of the bride didn't realize how beautiful she looked as she shared the stage with her daughter. It was sad she doubted herself so much. She had no faith in her gorgeous appearance or in her distinguished beauty, not only on the outside but also on the inside.

Story 2

"When dealing with people let us remember we are not dealing with peoples of logic. We are dealing with creatures of emotion people bursting with prejudices and motivated by pride and vanity." - Dale Carnegie

Beth remarked at the boldness of today's generation. "I wish I had their guts twenty-five years ago." She blurted. Upon further questioning, she confessed her anxiety during her children's childhood years.

Beth was busy and entangled in what was happening in the world around her. She laughed light heartedly, and a sparkle in her eyes brought back a time long past when her children were young.

Beth chose to breastfeed at a time when it was not accepted by the general population.

Many pediatricians were not knowledgeable about how, when, and where to feed the baby. You were on your own, Beth recalled. Her mother accepted it reluctantly, but her mother-in-law ostracized her. Beth had to go to a private room every time the baby needed to nurse. Michael Jordan considered his options and encourages us to do the same, "Obstacles don't have to stop you. If you run into a wall, don't turn around and give up. Figure out how to climb it, go through it, or work around it."

There were constant remarks about the baby's weight gain and ability to thrive on breast milk alone. When the baby would cry, the remarks would begin. "He must not be getting enough to eat," was the most common phrase used.

Beth was tired of hearing those words. At times, Beth would go home and replay everything and end up crying. It was an uphill battle. Every day she questioned if she were doing the right thing. The baby would appear to be so calm and relaxed after nursing Beth was sure she was doing what was best for the baby.

At other times when the baby would cry and fret, Beth wondered if she was doing anything correct. Her mother-in-law's constant barrage of unsupportive comments wore Beth's convictions. Being a new mother, she was unsure of herself, although she would never let it be known.

One day, Beth decided she should stop breast-feeding. She tried, but the baby would not accept the bottle. He was used to the breast and was not about to give it up so easily. Beth cried and began nursing him again. A friend had recently had a baby and was breast-feeding. Beth called this friend and sat down with her for a long talk. Beth gained a renewed sense of purpose and confidence which gave her the strength to continue breast-feeding. She was more successful the second time around.

Beth spent little time at her mother-in-law's to avoid the negative remarks. The baby was about two when Beth's husband asked and then made plans for them to visit overnight with his mother. Beth's second son was a few months old at that time. Beth was nursing him with more confidence. She now considered herself a pro, and she knew her first son had thrived on breast milk. Henry David Thoreau once said, "If one advances confidently in the direction of his dreams, and endeavors to live the life which he has imagined, he will meet with success unexpected in common hours."

The questioning of Beth's child rearing practices carried over into her toilet training method as well. Beth did not feel the need to rush her children to toilet train. When her son was two and her second son had just been born, Beth successfully got her two-year-old trained. She had not pushed him, but he was willing and able. Beth's mother-in-law had stated many times that her sons had not been easy to train. She expected Beth to experience a difficult time with her sons when she began toilet training. Such was not the case.

Beth was happy Paul was toilet trained. It made it easier to have only one child to change. Paul was just two years old but bright and attentive. Beth packed Paul's training pants so he could put them on during the night. He had not had any accidents, but it was not her house or crib, and she did not want to take any chances.

Beth was not looking forward to the visit, but it was something her husband wanted to do. They arrived at her mother-in-law's late at night. Beth swiftly got the baby ready for bed and then began tucking her two-year-old toddler into bed. Her mother-in-law was helping. When Beth did not place a diaper on him, her mother-in-law panicked. "He's only two, he'll wet the bed," she said. Beth answered in a relaxed manner that he would not wet the bed and that he was trained. Beth hoped her young son did not prove her wrong.

Nothing more was said, but the next morning when Paul began to cry to get out of bed, Beth's mother-in-law Kathy rushed to get him. Kathy quickly led him to the bathroom and helped him peel off the foot pajamas. Kathy could be heard from behind the bathroom door. "You didn't wet your pants," she yelled. Beth was on the other side of the door smiling.

Kathy had made many references to her own sons' toilet training days and the difficulty she had encountered. When Kathy and Paul emerged from the bathroom, Kathy hugged Beth and remarked, "Wow, my grandson is already trained. He is amazing." Beth smiled but wished her mother-in-law had trusted her in the first place when she said Paul was toilet trained. In the end, it wasn't important because both women learned something that day and became closer as a result. Each supported the other and a strained relationship transformed into a trusting one.

Discussion 2

"Forgiveness is the final form of love." - Reinhold Niebuhr

Beth retold the story in a more forgiving manner. It was in the past and had no consequence to the present. Beth only regretted she hadn't spoken to her mother-in-law years ago instead of allowing their relationship to erode in the beginning. Presently, both women walked on firm ground and relished their loving relationship.

It is difficult for most of us to accept there are many ways to do things and all of them are okay. Various roads lead to the same destination, yet when diverse methods to child rearing are instigated, it becomes offensive. One technique is not the only correct method. Respecting an individual's right to do what they consider the best option is one of the hardest things for people to accept. An anonymous person once gave us these words to consider: "Do not think you are on the right road just because it is a well beaten path."

There are many adults who manage to become adults through the various methods of their respective parents. Most adults do not remember what age they ate whole food or what age they toilet trained or took their first steps. Most people probably don't care. Making trivial things mountains will only separate us on either side of that mountain. Self-esteem is more important than flaunting an ego. Closeness is achieved when people work together and share ideas, pain, and happiness. Friedrich Nietzsche understood the double edged sword of communication when he said, "All things are subject to interpretation. Whichever interpretation prevails at a given time is a function of power and not truth."

Reflections for Mothers-in-Law

- Paying to have certain jobs done alleviates stress and time for your son and daughter-in-law.

- A man's first responsibility is to his wife and children. It is crucial to accept this.

- It is essential to wait and be grateful for any services your son provides.

- Guilt is not meant to be used as a tool of coercing your son into doing a job for you.

- Your son and daughter-in-law need space to resolve their own dilemmas.

- Respect the daughter-in-law's opinions and ideas on all subjects.

- Love is not diminished when it is given to others. It multiplies every time it is shared.

- It is fast and easy to see the faults. It is more virtuous to search for the good.

"Energy and persistence conquer all things."
- Benjamin Franklin

Questions for Mothers-In-Law

- Are you asking your son to do too many jobs for you?

- Are you aware offering advice about decisions and plans your son and daughter-in-law have already made is interference?

- When waiting for your son to do a job, do you mention calling a specialist to quicken his response or cause him to feel guilty?

- Do you engage your daughter-in-law during discussions in order to persuade her or prove her wrong?

- Are you happy to see your son or daughter-in-law when they call or visit rather than allude to how long it's been since you last heard from them?

- Do you let your daughter-in-law choose the restaurant when going to lunch?

- Are you flexible with a last minute change of plans?

Chapter 2 – Triumph and Defeat

*"You don't have the power to make life 'fair,'
but you do have the power to make life joyful."*
- Jonathan Lockwood Huie

There are many colors of paint in the store, and the colors are a reflection of the various partialities people have. If stores recognize the limitless expressions people develop, it is an easy task to respect another's preferences.

Respect can carry over into every aspect of our lives. Some people choose to dust their homes every day while others choose to do it once a year. If a son and daughter-in-law may choose to clutter their home, they should be allowed to let clutter reign. Some people like and own an animal. Any judgements are unwarranted.

Role-playing and role-changing display the freedom that is endowed. This liberty is important and necessary. The pleasure of accepting help when needed and refusing help when it is not needed is vital. When sons and daughters-in-law visit, they can freely express what is on their minds. They will be less apt to check their watches, anxiously contemplating departure time.

One couple views independence as being expressive about sharing household tasks. Each of the spouse's might exhibit control in their own sphere of preference. If the couple is happy with the rules, and the marriage is working they must be doing something right.

Consider what is envisioned when they buy a house. The way chosen to raise children is distinct. Some women choose to go back to work immediately after a baby is born. Providing their child or children with day care is a distressful necessity. Many women might be the sole providers and don't have the luxury of a choice. Mothers-in-law can't offer solutions to issues that have already been decided by the couple. Making suggestions on decisions already made only causes the couple frustrations.

Being independent is being allowed to select a workable decision to continue with one's career or stay at home with children. Mothers who work may be offended by the reproach of others. Mothers-in-law must not judge their daughters-in-law's choices. Some husbands are more supportive and make returning to work easier for the wife while others leave the brunt of childcare to their wives.

Some mothers choose to stay home. Sometimes being unconventional might require us to acknowledge the independent selections of another. This compels us to respect other people just as Socrates reveals, "The secret of change is to focus all of your energy not on fighting the old but on building the new."

The most difficult task for grooms is to convince their mothers, who have probably helped furnish and set up their first apartments, to step back or basically back off. Some mothers think about how they had just been called upon for a simple recipe or repair issue. Now the freedom has ended. Stopping by for a quick visit is not allowed.

The daughter-in-law does not want her mother-in-law observing the overflowing bucket, overfilled laundry basket or the dirty dishes in the sink, whatever the case may be. Understanding we all deal with similar situations allows us to refrain from commenting. Lao Tzu put it simply, "I have just three things to teach: simplicity, patience, compassion and these three are your greatest treasures."

The more a mother-in-law doesn't "notice" the more likely she is to develop bonds with a daughter-in-law who is made to feel at ease. There should be no guilt bestowed or insinuated. However, if the mother-in-law chooses to recognize and acknowledge every careless mistake she witnesses, she will most likely be relegated to scheduled visits.

The Queen and the Princess

If anyone chooses perfection, they will probably be disappointed. Enjoying people sometimes means accommodating the imperfections. In time the walls and barriers come down. Gordon B. Hinckley advocated looking for the positive in life with his response, "I am suggesting that as we go through life, we 'accentuate the positive.' If by looking deeper the good is found, then the voices of insult and sarcasm are stopped and we more generously compliment and endorse virtue and effort."

Nothing is more detrimental to a relationship than a daughter-in-law so overwhelmed by her mother-in-law she feels she must strike back at her mother-in-law with criticism. A husband's bad habits become the fault of his mother. The mother-in-law is seen as the person who raised him and made him messy, sloppy, and without table manners.

By berating her mother-in-law, a daughter-in-law feels less anxious about competing with her mother-in-law. Mothers-in-law must perceive and have a handle on the need to remain silent and allow their daughters-in-law to blossom at their own rate. Your daughter-in-law will work things out when she is more secure in her self-worth and ready to let go of any fears. Confidence grows slowly, so taken from the Richard Carlson book Don't Sweat the Small Stuff, one should ask the question; "Will this matter a year from now?"

Story 3

"How would your life be different if...You stopped making negative judgmental assumptions about people you encounter? Let today be the day... You look for the good in everyone you meet and respect their journey."
   - Steve Maraboli

Maggie sat up in bed admiring her new daughter. Her husband Jason and mother-in-law Trish were at her side. Maggie was beaming. She had such a hard time getting pregnant she thought they would never have children. She was ecstatic as she handed baby Elise to the nurse. After the nurse took Elise to the nursery, Maggie confronted Trish with a question. She asked Trish if she could baby-sit two days out of the week.

Trish was astounded. Her face flushed. Trish had just assumed that Maggie would stay at home with the baby for a little while. Trish reluctantly agreed, but she was noticeably shaken and upset. Her brand new granddaughter was going to be in daycare. Trish could hardly believe it   Trish was so fond of Maggie. It was Maggie who had nursed her through her own surgery a couple of years back. Maggie was strong. She did her own thing, as Trish loved to say. How could Maggie just go back to work and leave her young daughter. Trish shook her head as she looked at her son Jason who glanced back at his wife, sheepishly aware of what his mother was thinking. Trish argued with her son Jason all the way home. She made it a point that she'd stayed at home with him. Jason gripped the wheel of the car and tensed his body. He wished his mother would just be quiet. His wife Maggie had made a decision. Jason knew when Maggie made up her mind it was like a brick wall. Trish was not an unkind person but none of the current child issues were her concern. She might take the advice of Albert Schweitzer, "Little of the great cruelty shown by men can really be attributed to cruel instinct. Most of it comes from thoughtlessness or inherited habit."

Maggie decided to go back to work, and that was what she was going to do. Maggie worried about money all of the time. They had more than enough, but Maggie had already planned college for Elise by opening a bank account. Maggie had grown up without a father. Money was scarce, and her mother had gone back to work out of necessity. Maggie feared being destitute. She wanted to guarantee that Elise would never have to worry about being poor. Maggie trusted Trish and was confident Elise would be in exceptional hands. Jason understood Maggie's fears to a point, but he believed she was overreacting a bit, although he did not admit this to his mother. Jason thought it best to keep quiet.

Jason brought his mother home and begged her to keep her feelings to herself. Trish grumbled as she got out of the car. It was easy for Jason to say, but he wasn't going to be the one doing the babysitting, although she was secretly ecstatic.

Jason rode home alone, questioning his wife's decision. His mother and his wife were both strong willed. He wasn't sure who was right or wrong. Jason was confused and agitated. He wanted the best for his daughter. What he questioned was what the best was. His mother always thought she had all of the right answers. Now all Jason could think about was Maggie's decision to go back to work. He hated to believe he was questioning his wife. Jason tossed all night and was extremely tired the next day. He dressed, ate, and left for the hospital. He prepared his argument with Trish as he drove. Jason had a lot of doubt himself.

Jason was tense and confused when he parked his car and climbed out of it. Jason could not get his mother's remarks out of his head. He really did not want to argue with Maggie, but his mother's thoughts continued to play in his mind. He entered Maggie's room and stiffly stood. There was no hint of a smile, just a blank stare, from Maggie. As Maggie tipped her head and wrinkled her eyebrows, Jason blurted out that maybe she should stay at home with the baby for a while. Maggie frowned, and then laughed. "You've been talking to your mother," she blurted. Maggie and Jason talked for hours. Jason's fears were somewhat allayed, but he was still not convinced Maggie's resolution was the right one.

Maggie was inflexible. Jason would have to accept Maggie's judgement and lay his mother's fears to rest. Maggie loved Trish, and she adored her husband. She had no doubt both of them would come around. She smiled as she reflected on how fortunate she was to have a mother-in-law she loved and understood.

Discussion 3

Questioning each other's decisions appears to be relentless. Maggie made a decision that was right for her. It was her choice to make. Jason may give his input, but Maggie has to evaluate her own time management. Although on the surface this appears to be no concern to the mother-in-law, one must consider she will be doing the babysitting. Trish needs to accept to babysit or decline the offer. The couple is content with their decision, and Trish should not undermine the ruling. Jason is left with doubts because of his mother's fears and interference. The world, people, jobs and society encounter changes. A new generation has its own ideas on many subjects. The important thing is for the baby to receive love and attention from her parents.

Trish pressured the couple by interfering with a shared decision. Until Trish voiced her concerns, Jason was content with Maggie's choice. The time and circumstances were different when Trish was at home with Jason. It would not be a good thing for a woman to stay at home with her children if she is not satisfied. It will be detrimental to the children. If the mother is depressed and anxious, her ability to nurture will be in jeopardy. Likewise, if a mother is forced to return to work against her desires, she can become depressed. This will affect her work. Individual attitudes, personalities, and attributes can't be denied.

Reflections for Mothers-in-Law

- When your daughter-in-law can freely speak without criticism, her voice will be heard more often.

- Variety in soup makes it interesting, and that knowledge should be applied to living.

- The son and daughter-in-law's plan for a working relationship may differ from the one you and your husband share.

- Your daughter-in-law's child rearing may contrast with the methods you used. Many roads lead to success when done with love.

- Approaches to housecleaning and spending money are a personal matter.

- A reproachful attitude may cause your daughter-in-law to rudely defend herself.

- Applaud your daughter-in-law's efforts.

- Accept our diverse homes of origin impact every area of our lives.

- Married couples should not have to dodge questions or discuss future plans. This includes when or if they want a baby.

- No input from outside sources is required.

Questions for Mothers-in-Law

- Are you always challenging your daughter-in-law's opinions?
- Do you offer approvals or disapprovals of your daughter-in-law's decisions?
- Can you reflect before attempting to convince your son that your daughter-in-law's ideas are bad?
- Do you make your daughter-in-law feel uncomfortable in your presence?
- Do you try to persuade her to do what you think is best?

"Use what talents you possess; the woods would be very silent if no birds sang except those that sang best." - Henry Van Dike

Chapter 3 – Holiday Crises

"I don't need a holiday or a feast to feel grateful for my children, the sun, the moon, the roof over my head, music, and laughter, but I like to take this time to take the path of thanks less traveled." - Anonymous

Before the holidays are near, the anxiety is overwhelming. The reality of the experience differs from person to person, but any negative thinking ruins the holiday and creates havoc.

A good time is wanted by the entire family. Hurting the mother-in-law or daughter-in-law has a disastrous effect on the son or husband. It takes only one person to make or break the happy mood. Every holiday is different, but love can always be present. Attitude adds a dimension to the event. Carrying grudges to a holiday gathering promotes an antagonistic atmosphere. Some people wait for the opportunity to attack or set up the stage for it to happen.

When something weighs heavily on our minds, we should think before speaking. More thought makes it less attractive to speak unkindly. Too much credit is given to discussions behind closed doors. Most people have too much work to do and enough stress to keep them busy. Inconsequential disputes don't appear to be as important when the party is over. It makes us thankful the angry words were not spoken.

The daughter-in-law has a family and cherishes spending time with them. It is not an issue of debate. She might anticipate visiting her family on the holidays. She might be more anxious to see them if they live at a distance. The nicest gift you might give to your daughter-in-law is your blessing to go to her first family. The remembrances of holidays are not based on who did what for us but rather on how people made us feel.

Holiday Crises

The enjoyment of visiting with others throughout the year cannot be underestimated. If the mother-in-law cannot spend a holiday with the son and his family, she can make plans to get together at another date in the near future. Coming together and sharing gifts, food, and time is what the motive is. That can be accomplished at any time of the year. The important thing is to make sure a special time is scheduled. The holidays are a short period of time. It is the people who make the holiday special. Promote your own relationship of family love with your son and daughter-in-law. It can be a day at the beach with a picnic and stop for dinner. The ideas are endless.

Holiday time is confusing for everyone. Expectations are high, and the majority of people are inescapably disappointed when the holidays fail. We have a limited command of our lives. Recognizing the pitfalls of the holiday season does not ensure all family members will have a wonderful day. It is essential that everyone make their own enjoyment. Attitude is a key factor. When the added burden of the holidays is recognized, it helps to alleviate the pressure of contending with in-laws. Be grateful for what you have, including those in-laws. This anonymous quote tells an important reminder, "Having somewhere to go is HOPE, having someone to love is FAMILY, having both is a BLESSING."

Most couples facilitate discussions and conflicts, about where to spend a holiday, especially if travel is a consideration. The daughter-in-law may have young kids, which will make it harder to travel. Once a resolution has been made, the plans are constructed. When men agree with their wives' arrangement, peace and harmony are promoted. It might appear irresponsible of the husband to remain neutral, but if compliance results in a peaceful holiday, this is a troubleshooting solution.

"My idea of Christmas, whether old-fashioned or modern, is very simple: loving others. Come to think of it, why do we have to wait for Christmas to do that?" - Bob Hope

Duress by the mother-in-law is not going to make the situation easier. It might only cause resentment and future friction. Perhaps the mother-in-law would be encouraged if she had a date on the calendar to share with her son and his family. Postponing a dinner date for a future time will be more enjoyable. It is not about winning or losing but having a chance to spend time with family.

Visiting

"Wherever there is a human being, there is an opportunity for kindness."
- Seneca

Whatever the issues, couples have a difficult time deciding where they will attend a holiday. We all search for time to spend with our own families. Trying to schedule time with in-laws can become a battleground. If there is fighting between the couple prior to the visit, it will be reflected in the attitudes the couple displays.

Some parents may pressure their children to spend the holidays with them. If the son or daughter-in-law is from a smaller family, it impacts the decision. When the husband or wife is the only child, it complicates the choices further. Spending time with family throughout the year is an alternative choice that works for many people. Designated time for a family gathering any time of the year is what counts.

When siblings live at a distance and cannot be counted upon to entertain parents, this will also influence a couples' judgment. They may feel compelled to accept the burden and entertain their parents or to be present at their parents' house. Nothing might be said, but considerable is assumed. A daughter-in-law might want to spend time with her mother-in-law yet she understands her commitments to her family are undisputable. By now, we have an exhausted couple, possibly with erupting tempers.

The optimal circumstances are those that are the fairest, but fairness is thrown out the window when complications arise. A good compromise is essential, but not executed as often as it should be. When some form of compromise and peace is established, people enjoy the holidays a great deal more.

When Daughters-In-Law Visit

"How much pain has cost us the evils that have never happened."
- Thomas Jefferson

When a daughter-in-law ventures to spend the holidays with her mother-in-law, she has her own worries and anxieties. She is burdened with fears of being crushed, ignored, and controlled. A daughter-in-law may be apprehensive when she needs to be excused from the dinner table to take care of a baby or toddlers' needs. She doesn't want to ruin the dinner, but she can't ignore the baby or young child's requirements. Being receptive to the interruptions of a baby or toddler is extremely important for the mother-in-law. She can accommodate with a smile.

An understanding mother-in-law will provide a lot of space and a lot of rule bending if she wants to have future visits with her grandchildren. In the future, the daughter-in-law will deliberate before accepting another dinner invitation from her mother-in-law if she felt uncomfortable. A mother-in-law should recall the busy disruptive years of raising children and show consideration towards her daughter-in-law. Aldous Huxley said, "Most human beings have an almost infinite capacity for taking things for granted." The daughter-in-law must not assume her mother-in-law is upset about things that she may not be upset about.

A daughter-in-law may unwillingly accept a mother-in-law's pet because saying no to pets can exacerbate the mother-in-law's life or force her to stay home. Acquiescing to the presence of pets produces additional work for the daughter-in-law. It also affords its own assemblage of complications. Restraining the pet and keeping him away from the children unless told otherwise is crucial.

Pets should not freely roam another's home. Your daughter-in-law's home is no exception no matter how willing and accommodating she might be. When grandparents visit the grandchildren, they should make an effort to dwell on the positive. A negative attitude might distance the grandparents from their grandchildren's lives, although this is extreme. George Santayana reminds us with the words, "Our dignity is not in what we do, but what we understand." Daughters-in-law likely don't want to distance the grandparents and the grandparents don't want to lose touch with their grandchildren.

Another consideration is a mother-in-law's traveling companion. She may have a close male or female friend who accompanies her. The predicament mounts concerning the sleeping arrangements. If there are young children involved, a mother-in-law's discretion is imperative. This person may be a close friend to the mother-in-law, but they are a stranger to the rest of the family. Overcoming these dilemmas can be demanding. Any help one's daughter-in-law displays should not be underestimated.

Children complicate the situation in other ways. Grandparents want to see the children at holiday times. Grandparents have the potential to induce the couples' compliance. Thinking of gifts as contemplated abstract ideas may alleviate dissatisfaction. It is possible that our gifts to others are as much of a disappointment to them as their gifts are to us. Most often people purchase items they themselves would enjoy. What we cherish is not what another treasures.

If the gifts are not yielding sentiment, reconsider the way the gifts are selected. Gifts are not vouchers to be used at a later time. Perhaps gifts imply respect and warmth for someone. Khalil Gibran considered that time and effort were the best gifts with his words of wisdom, "You give but little when you give of your own possessions. It is when you give of yourself that you truly give."

Sometimes a gift may appear thoughtless and clueless but stems from the heart. Most gifts are sincere and should be accepted with gratitude. When people receive a gift, they should be thankful and trust in the honesty of the giver. Attempting to judge a gift is impractical. When your daughter-in-law stops to visit, invites you for dinner, runs an errand, or asks you to lunch, consider yourself blessed.

Story 4

"Life is simply time given to man to learn how to live. Mistakes are always part of learning. The real dignity of life consists in cultivating a fine attitude towards our own mistakes and those of others."- William Jordan

Stephanie was married to Steve. They had no children. Stephanie came from a large family and loved to cook. Her house was organized and clean at all times. Stephanie enjoyed sewing and needlepoint as well as all kinds of crafts. She consistently invited friends and family to dinner and set her table with matching color and décor. It was an experience to have dinner at her house.

Stephanie's mother-in-law, Karen, hated to cook. She bought frozen meals and opened canned vegetables for dinner. The extent of her cooking was a burger in the frying pan. Karen was thrilled whenever Stephanie invited her for dinner. Stephanie enjoyed cooking for her mother-in-law and invited her to dinner often. Karen always remarked how delicious Stephanie's homemade bread tasted. One day, Stephanie made a mental note to purchase a bread-maker for her mother-in-law. Stephanie lived up to the quote by Mother Theresa "Love begins at home, and it is not how much we do...but how much love we put in that action," with her own thoughtful actions.

On Mother's Day, Stephanie had the opportunity to present her mother-in-law with the bread maker. Stephanie anticipated a delighted reaction from her mother-in-law. Karen opened the gift and flashed angry glares at everyone. Karen was dissatisfied and gave harsh, negative remarks to Stephanie. Karen shoved the gift back into the box and rigidly handed it to Stephanie. Karen questioned Stephanie about her reasoning for purchasing the gift.

Although Stephanie attempted to recite her arguments, Karen was resistant to all Stephanie had to say. Karen ceased all discussion and petitioned Stephanie to return the gift. Karen considered the gift as an insult. She even suggested Stephanie might keep the gift for herself.

Stephanie was crushed. She was deeply aware of how hurtful her gift appeared to be when her mother-in-law exhibited such a demonstration of poor behavior. Stephanie deduced how much her mother-in-law hated to cook. Stephanie concluded her mother-in-law could still have homemade bread by tossing ingredients into the machine. It required little effort Stephanie thought. Stephanie was left without any options. The next week she returned her mother-in-law's gift. Both women were discouraged and unhappy. Their once solid relationship now had some cracks.

"That best portion of the good man's life-his little namelessness, unremembered acts of kindness and of love." - Wadsworth.

Discussion 4

"When you practice gratefulness, there is a sense of respect toward others. When you are discontent, you always want more, more, more. Your desire can never be satisfied. But when you practice contentment, you can say to yourself, 'Oh yes - I already have everything that I really need.' " - Dalai Lama

It was clear that Stephanie enjoyed cooking and would relish any kitchen object she received. The mistake Stephanie made was buying Karen something she would have liked to obtain for herself. Stephanie's aim was honorable because she wanted her mother-in-law to enjoy homemade bread even when her mother-in-law did not take pleasure in cooking. Stephanie aspired to save her mother-in-law the time and effort involved in bread making yet reward her with delicious results.

Karen did not see Stephanie's point of view. Karen assessed Stephanie's purchase as thoughtless. Karen assumed if Stephanie had considered her needs, she would have recalled she was not a cook or a baker. Stephanie did not anticipate the effect of the gift. Both women were unable to communicate their thoughts clearly. Both were deeply wounded. Before giving the machine to her mother-in-law, Stephanie might have explained the simplicity of using the appliance and procuring the benefits. This might have allayed Karen's fears in operating the mechanism.

It is most important to consider what behavior a person reveals towards us more than a token gift they give to us. The intangible demeanor may reflect the inner feelings more than the tangible souvenirs. Stephanie's gift was extremely thoughtful and Karen's attitude was deplorable in many ways. Of course, Stephanie might have thought it through a bit more, but Karen could have attempted to understand the reasoning behind the gift. In the future, they might be able to talk things over to grasp each other's sentiments.

Reflections for Mothers-in-Law

- Remember your daughter-in-law has a family she wants to spend time with.

- Holidays can have good and bad memories.

- We remember who did what for us quicker than who gave what to us.

- It is fun to visit with family throughout the year, not just at holiday time.

- Don't compare yourself to your daughter-in-law's mother. You can be a friend.

- Each holiday is unique. Accept the new holiday traditions, and make other plans for visits with the family.

- Most of us choose a gift we want. Be grateful for your gifts, trusting they were given with love.

- When your son and his wife feel comfortable, they will return and visit more often.

- We remember any occasion by how others made us feel.

Questions for Mothers-in-Law

- Are you supportive when your son and his wife share a holiday with her family?

- Do you refrain from complaining about your daughter-in-law's gift and consider the positive motives she might have had?

- Are there obligations you must do when your daughter-in-law does a favor for you?

- Are you willing to change any of your traditions if it results in peace?

- Do you place as much importance on sharing a summer day with your son and daughter-in-law as you do sharing a holiday with them?

- Are you careful about the gifts you buy for your daughter-in-law as you believe she should be about the gifts she buys for you?

Chapter 4 – Money Misery

"There's only one corner of the universe you can be certain of improving, and that's your own self." - Aldous Huxley

Money is vital to our survival. It can be used to influence, control, and gain material possessions. Money might be used as a wedge or bartering tool. It is difficult to compete with a device that can be used as an authoritative weapon. Money commands and enforces. Innocent people can easily get caught in its web. It has the potential to promise, indulge, gratify, and corrupt.

Money has the power to motivate others for the benefit of one's own good. The person holding the wealth is the only winner. Most often, the use of money as leverage is compelling, and although people love receiving monetary gifts, it limits the appreciation from others. In a way, both the giver and receiver are hurt. Money cannot buy respect.

A mother-in-law should understand that bestowing money on her son and daughter-in-law may never manifest more than a thank you. It is a mistake to give a gift with conditions. Reciprocation likely is not in any plan. Awareness to the situation should alleviate expectations. The best gift is the one with no "strings" attached. Love does not make us duty bound and cannot be bought.

Another hazard of lending money is the real or imagined debt placed on the married couple. A mother-in-law might make more demands on the young couple because she has confidence in the fact that they owe her. It makes it necessary to request help from the son humbly. There is a difference in the way a person requests aid. The mother-in-law might say, "Can you come this weekend and help me with the yard because I really want to get it done right

Money Misery

away?" It might be better if she says, "I know I lent you money, so if you have other plans, don't feel obligated. However, if you could help me with the back yard for about an hour this weekend, I would appreciate it," He may be more receptive to the later request of help. As said by Papyrus "A man who has taken your time recognizes no debt, yet it is the only debt he can never repay."

Reflections for Mothers-in-Law

- Keep your gifts of money sincere so you are not giving as a means to an end.

- Allow your son and daughter-in-law time to repay any money they have borrowed without a constant reminder.

- Consider any time your daughter-in-law gives you more precious than a gift of money. Time is more precious a gift.

- Accept your daughter-in-law's right to do what she wants with any gift she receives from you.

- If your daughter-in-law is comfortable when she visits, she will be relaxed and more apt to share her thoughts.

- Your wealth should never be used to control or subdue your daughter-in-law.

- Money should never be used to boast, brag, belittle, or manipulate others.

- Never allow your grandchildren to equate your money gifts with your love for them.

Questions for the Mother-in-Law

- Do you consider you might be wrong when you think your daughter-in-law's gifts are thoughtless?

- Do you like your daughter-in-law's gifts more when you know the cost?

- Are you placing pressure on your son and daughter-in-law to help you with tasks because you gave them a large monetary gift?

- Have you ever questioned your daughter-in-law's appreciation for gifts and money?

- Do you keep a tally of what you and your daughter-in-law give to each other?

- Do you give unconditional love to your son and daughter-in-law and reflect on what that means?

Chapter 5 – Jealousy Is Poisonous

"Take two kids in competition for their parents' love and attention. Add to that the envy that one child feels for the accomplishments of the other; the resentment that each child feels for the privileges of the other; the personal frustrations that they don't dare let out on anyone else but a brother or sister, and it's not hard to understand why in families across the land, the sibling relationship contains enough emotional dynamite to set off rounds of daily explosions." - Adele Faber

A mother-in-law may feel animosity towards her daughter-in-law because of the attention her son gives to his wife. A mother-in-law may dislike how much attention her daughter-in-law bestows on her own mother. Mothers-in-law might appear to favor their daughter's children over their son's children. It is not actually essential if these are fact or fiction if the daughter-in-law perceives these fixations as reality. Recognizing jealousy is one aspect, but overcoming the emotional confusion of jealousy is no minor accomplishment.

Inadvertently, a mother-in-law might upset her daughter-in-law by volunteering to come to her son's aid. The truth is the daughter-in-law might refuse any attempts the mother-in-law makes to help. If a mother-in-law continues to offer support, she can be seen as interfering. This might be as simple an occurrence as the mother-in-law getting her son a cup of coffee or changing his baby for him when it's his turn to do it. There are few times when a mother can help the adult son, so when an opportunity occurs, she might leap at the chance to give assistance. She is unaware of the consequences the actions incur. It is not wise for a man to place his mother before his wife, although each woman holds a special place in his heart.

The mother-in-law can offer support in a manner her daughter-in-law suggests. In that way, the mother-in-law is not in the middle, and she is able to help out. She might also be able to do more for her son when she is recognized as a team player. As Sunshine Magazine said, "Doubtless, it is a human frailty. But most of us, in the glow of feeling we have pleased, want to do more to please and knowing we have done well, want to do better." These kindnesses build trust and freedom.

Son Praises Wife

"Life has taught me that it is not for our faults that we are disliked and even hated, but for our qualities." - Bernard Berenson

Mothers-in-law are obliged to remember to refrain from judging their daughters-in-law. A mother-in-law may destroy her daughter-in-law when she refuses to overlook anything or compromise at all. The daughter-in-law is a vital component in her son's life. This woman is the one the son selected as the recipient of his true love. She is or possibly will be the mother of his children. Perpetual disapproval results in emotional suffering. They will keep their distance even though your son may always love you. He will not be able to cope with the persistent assault on his wife.

Active aggression is erroneous, but being passively aggressive is also a mistake. It is worthwhile to avoid discussing your son's former girlfriends. This could be viewed as a deliberate act of passive aggression. Even mentioning earlier girlfriends in his life can provoke anger. It can be offensive to your son's wife. It initiates a stressful situation for your son. All people have faults, and past girlfriends are no exception. They were just as imperfect as the woman he married, but they did not become the daughter-in-law.

A mother-in-law may be envious of the attention her son gives his wife. The reasons for this jealousy may be multifaceted.

Jealousy thrives everywhere, and nobody is immune. Lack of attention may be what drives anyone to resentment. When a person exhibits a jealous attitude, it can imply they lack confidence in themselves. It can make a person want to swiftly tear that person down as was written in a Sanskrit Proverb, "Men soon learn the fault of others, and some discover virtues. But is there one I have a doubt who can discern his own defects?"

They do not recognize the hardships, agony, or pain others have had to endure. It is possible many of us may be distrustful of factors that are not even real. Sometimes it forces the person to have faith in the facts of the situation, but we could be mistaken. The wonderful things we notice on the exterior of a person might be purely surface facade. The pain, anguish, and worry another person suffers may be hidden from the view of others.

Most people would not switch places with anyone. If it happened, they would be gratified to get back to their own life's problems. It is essential to remember assumptions are never as they appear.

A mother-in-law should try to see beyond the visible world, taking the whole person into account and refusing to pass judgment. What one person accomplishes and values is subjective. Each person chooses their own approaches to life, and that is subjective. A mother-in-law must respect the way her children care to live. A daughter-in-law lacks some abilities, but the mother-in-law lacks other talents as well.

Setting goals that are impossible for others to attain is not wise. Each person should set their own goals. A trace of jealousy may always be present, but it can be kept in check. The struggle to balance our lives in peace can be challenging but not impossible. On the surface it can appear others have an easier life. Most people face many struggles, and some troubles are kept secret. Supporting each other with patience and respect can make life laid-back for everyone. It is possible to manage the jealous tendencies. Picture Quotes defined how easy it is to be disliked for our goodness, "I don't give anyone a reason to hate me. They create their own drama out of pure jealousy."

It is reasonable a daughter-in-law may enjoy her mother-in-law's company, but she is fearful of letting her mother-in-law get too close. She may feel she is betraying her own mother if she allows it to happen. It is just as important for the mothers of daughters to let go of the control and give some space and freedom. Thich Nhat Hanh said it was of great magnitude to find peace within when he said, "Our capacity to make peace with another person and with the world depends very much on our capacity to make peace with ourselves."

Narrow Minded Gossip

"It is just as cowardly to judge an absent person as it is wicked to strike a defenseless one. Only the ignorant and narrow-minded gossip, for they speak of persons instead of things." - Lawrence G. Lovasik

None of us like to be accused of gossiping. It is the most common form of recreation we all indulge in, no matter how old we are. Questioning the reasons for participating in the activity helps the person understand where the desire comes from. Many times, a person loses sight of the damage it causes. It appears to be harmless, so it is rarely stopped. In the end, one is left to feel shame and sorrow or guilt.

One may be stressed out with their daughter-in-law. Their mind tricks them into believing there are certain meanings present in their exchanges with their daughters-in-law. In fact, a derogatory meaning was never meant. It was just the way the remarks or actions were interpreted. If the mother-in-law is in a good disposition, she might just ignore the words or actions of her daughter-in-law and chuck it up to a bad day. We must admit gossiping hurts a real person. When it is an honest fact, it can still do damage to a person's image, just as Frank A. Clark said, "Gossip needn't be false to be evil there's a lot of truth that shouldn't be passed around."

Story 5

"God gave us minds to think with and hearts to thank with. Instead we use our hearts to think about the world as we would like it to have been, and we use our minds to come up with rationalizations for our ingratitude. We are a murmuring, discontented, unhappy, ungrateful people. And because we think we want salvation from our discontents…" - Douglas Wilson

Deb was happy for her son Pete and his wife Megan. They had given birth to their second child days ago. Their oldest child was a daughter. She was now two and quite a handful. Deb was a major asset to Megan. She helped with the babysitting throughout the pregnancy. Deb was always willing to give Megan a break. She also had them over for dinner often or sent meals over to them.

It was great having her son and daughter-in-law living close by. It allowed her the opportunity to lend a hand with things. Megan's parents lived out-of-state. After the baby was born, they came to visit with Megan. One day, Deb stopped by to visit Megan and the new baby, which Deb had not yet held. Diane, Megan's mother, was holding and rocking the baby. Deb took a seat and silently waited her turn to hold the baby. Diane made no offer to give her the baby. Megan was busy and paid no attention to her mother or mother-in-law. Two hours past, and Deb was anxious to get home. She had still not held the baby. Megan reached for her sleeping baby. Deb asked if she could hold her sleeping granddaughter. Megan replied the baby was tired, and she was going to put her in for a nap. The rebuff was like a slap in the face for Deb. She rose to leave, unable to face Diane or Megan. She was consequently dejected as she traveled back home, and Shannon Alder said it precisely, "I am tired of people saying that poor character is the only reason people do wrong things. Actually, circumstances cause people to act a certain way. It's from those circumstances that a person's attitude is affected followed by weakening of character. Not the reverse. If we had no faults of our own, we should not take so much pleasure in noticing those in others and judging their lives as black or white, good or bad. We all live our lives in shades of gray."

Deb complained to her son. Her son replied he assumed she enjoyed doing things for them, and he did not know they were inconveniencing her as Deb implied. Deb was even more frustrated. She had not meant to sound like a whining person. Deb did enjoy doing things for her son and daughter-in-law, but now her son thought she didn't. Deb was feeling worse by the minute. She regretted having spoken at all and just couldn't find the correct words that could remedy the situation she found herself in. Deb did not feel appreciated. She felt used. Now her son and daughter-in-law assumed she did not enjoy her grandchildren. Deb was anxious and stressed.

Discussion 5

"The marvelous richness of human experience would lose something of rewarding joy, if there were not limitations to overcome. The hilltop hour would not be half so wonderful if there were no dark valleys to traverse." - Helen Keller

Diane was probably aware of the fact her time with the baby was limited. She made no effort to allow Deb to hold the baby, because she knew Deb would have many opportunities to do so. Megan was so proud of her new daughter, and happy to have her mother visiting she basically ignored her mother-in-law.

The Queen and the Princess

Deb was displaying signs of jealousy towards Megan's mother, Diane. Deb could have waited the few days before attempting to visit with her new grandchild and it would have allowed Diane some quality time alone with her daughter and new granddaughter. Deb could visit with Megan after Megan's mother had gone home. As hurtful as this situation was for Deb, it was difficult for Megan and upsetting for Diane.

Megan was giving all of her attention to her own mother. One can appreciate the happiness that Megan was experiencing but she did ignore her mother-in-law who had been a positive presence throughout her pregnancy. It was hurtful to Deb and even if Deb had not been helpful during the pregnancy, she still deserved some attention and recognition as the other grandmother. Both the mother and the mother-in-law might have resolved the situation themselves by compromising. This would have taken the responsibility away from Megan who had to deal with the repercussions after the incident. Deb could have permitted Megan some private time with her mother and should have postponed her visit, or been happy to simply gaze at her new grandchild. Diane might have allowed Deb to hold the baby and then quickly snatched her right back. This would have saved face for Deb, allowed Megan a reprieve and honored Diane with the satisfaction of being the bigger person.

The baby is going to be around for a long time. There will be many other times to hold and rock the baby. Megan could have given Deb a few moments to hold the baby prior to Deb's departure. It is hard for most people to make quick decisions in challenging and awkward situations. Judging any of the three players serves no purpose except to do better the next time.

Diane is jealous of Deb's ten minute, close access to Megan and the baby. Living in another state places her further away from the daily activities. Deb is jealous of the control Megan's mother has on her daughter. Because Deb is willing to do the menial work, she believes this should entitle her to special privileges.

Megan is inexperienced at handling this difficult situation

in a fair manner. She does not know how to deal with her mother or mother-in-law when given a sticky situation. As much as she appreciates her mother-in-law, she loves her mother. Megan admitted doing nothing because she didn't want to hurt anyone's feelings but the tense atmosphere only intensified. Megan could have stated that it would be best for the mother-in-law to come back during the week, so that she would have more time to bond with the baby. Humor could have been added to alleviate the tension between the two older women. Humor is a great reliever of tension.

There is no point in making assumptions because most are wrong. The procedure chosen is considered briefly. It is later when the mistakes are discovered that the impetuousness is understood. It supports the theory of taking everything that is said and done as a half thought out message of truth.

"Everything has its wonders, even darkness and silence, and I learn whatever state I may be in, therein to be content." – Helen Keller

"The best and most beautiful things in the world cannot be seen or even touched. They must be felt within the heart." - Helen Keller

Reflections for Mothers-in-Law

- Your son loves his wife and she deserves respect from you which includes you never gossiping about her, especially behind her back.

- Your daughter-in-law plays a significant role in your life. She is struggling with her own issues and doing her best.

- Encourage your daughter-in-law and son to reach for dreams no matter how bizarre.

- Remember praise and gratefulness go a long way in healing hurts.

- Be above suspicion, and be someone your daughter-in-law may trust.

- Discussing your son's past girlfriends will erode his relationship with you.

- Respect and love all of your daughters-in-law and their children by not comparing.

- Never make assumptions about the daughter-in-law and hope she is not making assumptions about you.

- Never force your son to choose between you and his wife in any situation. Love increases when it is shared, and there is room for both of you in his heart.

Questions for the Mother-in-Law

- Do you think your daughter-in-law is spoiled by your son, and does it make you jealous?

- Do you make assessments about your grandchildren by noticing height, weight, academic or physical ability and beauty?

- Do you make your son crazy with questions about his wife?

- Do you compliment a grandchild for helping someone?

- Do you construe what is said to fit your own interpretation?

- Are you making too many assumptions about why your daughter-in-law says or does certain things?

- Are compassion and mindfulness considered as some of the top attributes of choice to have?

"Darkness cannot drive out darkness; only light can do that. Hate cannot drive out hate; only love can do that." - Martin Luther King.

Chapter 6 – Respect Mistakes

"Mistakes are a part of being human. Appreciate your mistakes for what they are: precious life lessons that can only be learned the hard way." - Al Franken

A mother-in-law's fairness to her daughter-in-law is partly out of consideration for her son. People offend others regularly with their unkind behaviors. It might be that most people are unaware of their practices. When someone is wounded, they respond back. This escalates a situation. When a person assumes things that are untrue mini, wars begin and end with more suffering. It takes common sense and an ability to have faith others are not trying to hurt us.

As long as someone believes something was done on purpose, it is difficult to change her mind. Many disagreements happen when a mother-in-law or daughter-in-law believes she was wronged. Jealousy and disharmony in relationships can be conceived in the mind and heart. Love is important, and people panic if they lose it. Everyone wants to be in first place, and it is almost impossible to shine at second. However, no one stops to recall why certain people are catered to or placed in a position of importance. I think the squeaky wheel syndrome is strong.

A mother-in-law might show consideration for her daughter-in-law by taking charge of the baby so that her daughter-in-law could get some needed rest. She might also be a sounding board by listening to the daughter-in-law's complaints. Helping a daughter-in-law cope with children is considerate. Judgements are subjective and should be recognized as that. A mother-in-law can reject the daughter-in-law's concepts without rejecting the daughter-in-law.

Respect Mistakes

Through observations, I found daughters-in-law complain when mothers-in-law unexpectedly visit. Daughters-in-law prefer a heads up when a mother-in-law will be visiting. The daughters-in-law complained they worked a full time job and had children to contend with. If they invited their mothers-in-law, they stated they did not cook much because they were not "gourmet cooks."

Some daughters-in-law stated they believed their mothers-in-law stopped by unexpectedly to spy on them and to catch them and their house in complete disarray. One daughter-in-law stated, "She just wants to check up on my housecleaning habits and cooking ability."

As told by the mother-in-law, it is also a no win situation. If they offer to help, it is denied, but the mother-in-law feels like a guest in her son's house because she is not allowed to give. In this situation, we are not being kind because there are times when allowing someone to be supportive are actually a thoughtful thing to do. So many people can feel useless when nobody lets them help. Most mothers-in-law want to help but worry about stepping over the line.

When both women state clearly what it is they want from each other, it becomes easier to meet in the middle. That is the place of residence for the man. The women tug opposite ways at the coat sleeve of the man in the middle. He is told what to say to his mother by his wife and what to say to his wife by his mother.

Unless the need to win and be right is released, the silent hidden battling continues. Life is a circle, and it comes around to us again in a different way. The daughter-in-law who doesn't explain her wants and needs may not be satisfied at her mother-in-law's house. If this is a way to keep her and the husband from going to his mother's house, then she will be successful. It is up to the mother-in-law to work for peace.

Nobody has to get wounded. The fabrication is drama, and it creates winners and losers and, honestly, nobody wants to be a loser. With a little reflection, we can become a bit kinder and more compassionate. In life we all play so many roles, and what might seem so far away is in front of us at daybreak. The way one wants to be treated should be reciprocated.

If a mother-in-law is trying to find imperfections, she will easily find them. The ability to ignore another's shortcomings is at the center. By being aware of another's struggles, we may connect on a higher level with that person and value their worth and effort.

The daughter-in-law should not be expected to produce a gourmet meal. Likewise, the daughters-in-law agreed that an unexpected visit now and again, was okay, provided their mother-in-law abstained from criticism.

The trouble with relationships is people hide so much of their feelings. That is not wise. The relationships are not real if we pretend all is well when we do not believe it in our hearts. When someone is unhappy, they need to honestly state their opinion. When a person accepts compromise by agreeing to disagree, they are choosing appreciation. This is far better than imagining we are on the same page at all times when it isn't reality.

Others can unwittingly destroy the seeds of self-esteem planted within us. If a person stops the judgements and fault-finding, it leaves room for a relationship to peacefully develop. Mothers-in-law and daughters-in-law are from different generations. There is room for the daughter-in-law to grow and develop and for the mother-in-law to accommodate new knowledge.

Mothers of boys must turn the torch over to the new woman in her son's life. This is not easy. This is not professing the mother-in-law has no right to ever speak plainly to her son again. It simply implies she recognizes the new union and defers to it. Sons will still trust and honor their moms, and daughters-in-law should respect that. If they want advice, they can ask for it and can say no if they do not want suggestions.

Some mothers-in-law freely admitted how happy they were with their sons wives. They felt it made it easier for them to let go of the reins when the wife was so caring towards her son. In the end, they knew they had no choice but to release their hold, and releasing them willingly was a wonderful feeling. Trust on both sides takes time, but it is worth the effort. Daughters-in-law are younger and haven't the experience to support some of their judgments, but a mother-in-law shouldn't allow age to be the judge.

Marriage is like a government overhaul. It is not easy to come through unscathed. Carl Jung remarked, "Nobody as long as he moves about among the accounts of life, is without trouble." We are rewarded with contentment and self-esteem. In the process, it is good to remember that we never lost love, we only multiplied love. Neither woman is more special than the other, but both have plenty to gain by sharing. Awareness is vital, as Oliver Wendell Homes observed, "A moment's insight is sometimes worth a life's experience."

Story 6

"Life is a series of events and sensations. Everything else is interpretation. Much is lost in translation and added in assumption / projection"
- Rasheed Ogunlaru

Sue, a mother-in-law for all of three years, was distraught because her daughter-in-law refused to buy furniture or curtains for her house. Sue also deemed her daughter-in-law's house cleaning effort poor. Her daughter-in-law Monica stated to Sue many times she wanted to wait and buy what she wanted when she had the money. Monica also said house cleaning was not a principal priority. She had more important things to do.

Sue took this as an affront. Sue considered herself an excellent housekeeper. She took pride in her beautiful house and in her attempts to keep her house neat and clean. The circumstances were distressing for both Monica and Sue.

Each had a sense of determination that was dissimilar from each other's. Sue was insulted by Monica's attitude towards keeping a house. Sue believed it was a reflection of the care her son Ben might be receiving.

In Monica's thinking, this could not be further from the truth. Monica understood she wasn't interested in performing mundane tasks that were unappealing. Monica also refused to clutter her house with trinkets she did not like and could not relate to. She had no problem waiting to buy what she wanted. She and her husband Ben would continue to sleep on the mattress that was on the floor until further notice.

Sue could not believe this situation. She shook her head and dejectedly surrendered by refusing to approach the subject again. This was a relief to Monica who sensed she finally was allowed a little reprieve. Unless we meet in the middle and compromise, peace will remain elusive. Muriel Barberry said it strongly, "We never look beyond our assumptions and what's worse, we have given up trying to meet others; we just meet ourselves."

Monica and her husband Ben did not have the money to purchase the more expensive furniture and curtains they preferred. Monica refused to buy cheaper items merely to have curtains on the windows or chairs in the kitchen. Monica was willing to postpone her purchase until they could afford to buy the expensive items she craved.

Sue was distraught. Her own home was immaculate and orderly. Monica enjoyed living in her home the way it was, which was disorganized and chaotic. Monica and Ben had no curtains on the windows and their mattress was as stated, thrown on the floor, but they were happy. Pillows were scattered on the floor to be used as seats. Ben and Monica were content to wait despite Sue's protests.

Sue's thoughts on the subject were entirely different. She believed Monica should put a lot more time into her homemaking effort. At one point, Sue became agitated. She viewed their home as a reflection of herself. This was a mistake. Sue was embarrassed for anyone in the family to visit Ben and Monica because of the craziness of their home.

One day, Sue decided to give Monica some discarded furniture and curtains. Sue also went to Monica's and cleaned the house from top to bottom. Sue believed that Monica would be so impressed that she would keep the house that way.

Monica reluctantly accepted the gifts and hung the curtains. After a month had past, the dog had ripped the bottom of the curtains to shreds. The dog had also chewed on the arms of the chairs.

When Sue stopped over for a visit, she could not believe her eyes. The house was in complete disarray. Sue was destroyed. Her relationship with her daughter-in-law deteriorated rapidly. Sue allowed false pride to rule her life and tried to instill this false pride in others.

Discussion 6

"We know what a person thinks not when he tells us what he thinks but by his actions." - Isaac Bashevis Singer

The saddest part of this story is the mother-in-law and daughter-in-law did not intentionally aspire to hurt each other, but they did. The daughter-in-law did not respect her mother-in-law's gifts. To her credit, she put up with her mother-in-law's continuous interference and insults. Out of respect, she may have accepted the furniture and curtains in good faith to please Sue. Ben and Monica always had dogs, and the damage they can do was obvious. Nobody encouraged the dogs to shred the curtains or chew on the couch.

Monica might have appreciated Sue's help with the cleaning, but she could not keep the house as neat and organized as Sue kept her house. Monica did not consider house cleaning a priority. Monica never fancied silly objects and never asked for them. Monica felt by taking Sue's gifts, she was initiating an atmosphere of respect and peace with Sue.

When Sue became upset with Monica, the anger and resentment Monica felt about the gifts exploded into wrath. Monica was pleased the dog ate the items because she was relieved of something she never wanted in the first place, and she resented her mother-in-law's interference. Monica should have refused the gifts.

Sue should not have forced her daughter-in-law to take the gifts. Sue should have considered Monica's point of view and respected her justification and patience towards the mother-in-law.

Once Sue gave the gifts to Monica, she had no right to dictate how Monica should handle them. The gifts could be used or abused as Monica desired. Sue wanted to improve Monica's house, but Monica was content and happy and never stressed over cleaning. In Proverb 12:25 it states clearly the value of a compliment, "Anxious hearts are very heavy, but a word of encouragement does wonders!"

We all have our own priorities, and they need to be respected. Sue expected her daughter-in-law to feel guilty about the way the gifts were abused when Sue lamented the torn curtains. Sue disregarded the fact Monica had not wanted the curtains but were forced on her. Monica wasn't arrogant, but she was independent. Jill Botte Taylor explained finding serenity amongst the stresses of life, "To experience peace does not mean that your life is always blissful. It means that you are capable of tapping into a blissful state of mind amidst the normal chaos of a hectic life."

Reflections for Mothers-in-Law

- If you share your thoughts with your daughter-in-law, she will have more insight, and you both walk on firmer ground.

- The mistakes we witness in others are clearly visible in us, but they are kept hidden.

- Do you believe your daughter-in-law misunderstands you on purpose so that you become the "Bad Guy"?

- Offer your items, your help, and your advice, but never use force. Accept no for an answer.

- When your daughter-in-law offers support, allow her to give it because we all like to be needed.

- Playing the martyr will get you attention and will help you win, but the cost is a loss of the son, grandkids, and daughter-in-law. The reverse is also true. Do we want the kids to have and know their grandparents?

- Can we give empathy and let go of the pettiness?

Questions for Mothers-in-Law

- Do we want to have disagreements and ultimatums that end up dissolving the relationship with the daughter-in-law?

- When the house is messy, do you give your daughter-in-law allowances or take notice?

- Is gossiping about your daughter-in-law something you engage in?

- Do you always have to be right when in a discussion with your daughter-in-law?

- Must you give your advice even when it is unwanted because you are older and wiser?

- Does it make you angry when your son and his wife don't follow your advice?

- Do you know when you have crossed the line and does it bother you?

- Can you remember when everything was new and exciting during the first years of marriage, and does it make it easier for you to understand your daughter-in-law?

- Do you strive for harmony or disputes, and do you want the grandkids to know you?

Chapter 7 - Overcome Fear

"What screws us up the most in life is the picture in our head of what it's supposed to be. If you don't get what you want, you suffer; if you get what you don't want, you suffer; even when you get exactly what you want, you still suffer because you can't hold on to it forever. Your mind is your predicament. It wants to be free of change. Free of pain, free of the obligations of life and death. But change is law and no amount of pretending will alter that reality."
- Socrates

Accepting individuality with graciousness allows diversity to govern our lives in harmony. When interpreting another's behaviors or expressions there is a multitude of explanations. Minds produce havoc on emotions and the truth gets lost.

Covering up, hiding, and embellishing whatever happens is done in order to compete against a perceived enemy. If people partake in this game, nobody wins. Everyone goes home defeated. No one can assume others are focusing attention on us. When what is said and done is distorted, misinterpretations are made. Hiding from faults portrays a false image. Being insecure produces a desire to be exact and be paid attention to.

Younger people are relevant and viable and have some self-worth. They feel competent at making decisions. The point is they will be the same person when they are older, just as we are still the same person. Allowing ourselves to be defined as a person by somebody else was a mistake. The definition is far removed from the person we are and the abilities we accumulated, through understanding the dive into despair is stopped. More compassionate words I cannot find than those spoken by Audrey Hepburn, "For beautiful eyes, look for the good in others; for beautiful lips, speak only words of kindness; and for poise, walk with the knowledge that you are never alone."

Our attitudes, looks, age, and personalities usually enter into decisions others make about us. One may not be able to control these matters. Our ability to control our own beliefs is strong, and our character is known to us and a higher being. Building our self-confidence and trust is defining us. Our worthiness as individuals deserving respect is supreme.

Fluidity of Pride and Status

"The battle you are going through is not fueled by the words or actions of others; it is fueled by the mind that gives it importance." - Shannon L. Alder

Insecurity hinders our ability to praise the capabilities of others. It might stop us from paying tribute to them because of our constant attention to our own underlying pride. Uncertainty leaves us craving to be the focus of attention. It appears silly to be threatened by another's ability.

A mother-in-law may not listen to a daughter-in-law's advice because she fears being overshadowed. A mother-in-law or daughter-in-law perhaps disparages each other's attempts to flourish, submerged in their own uncertainties.

The mother-in-law and daughter-in-law are unjustified in their concern regarding how much they are valued by their son/husband. It is likely the assessment the husband/son makes pertaining to his mother or wife fosters in them merit or demerit.

A son's reassurance to his mother decreases her fearfulness of losing him. Developing her self-esteem enhances her freedom and confidence. It helps her to release her grip on her son.

Strength in Challenges

"When we long for life without difficulties, remind us that oaks grow strong in contrary winds and diamonds are made under pressure." - Peter Marshall, Scottish clergyman

It is difficult to be the friend of an insecure person because they presume everyone wishes to outwit them. They are hesitant of favors and skeptical of the intentions. They cannot relax their guard. It is difficult to nurture a relationship in such an atmosphere. Gaining the trust of a cynic is probably difficult but not impossible. It preconditions patience and understanding as well as an acceptance of their cautious nature.

Confidence in our abilities subdues controversial beliefs that plague a mother-in-law or daughter-in-law. The consequences of too many assumptions might result in off-base conjectures. Disregarding tactless remarks instead of lashing out in retaliation is the better course of action. A person may deliberate before speaking and be attentive to what is expressed. Trust goes a long way in promoting peace and harmony.

Story 7

"Life is no brief candle to me. It is a sort of splendid torch which I have got hold of for the moment, and I want to make it burn as brightly as possible before handing it on to future generations." - George Bernard Shaw

Barbara is married to Charlie. She is a composed and confident woman. She and Charlie now live in a condo and both are pleased with the arrangement. Barbara is quick to allude to her past and lack of confidence. She began to retell her story anxiously. She recalled her frail ego and vulnerability when she and Charlie were first married. It was a second marriage for her and a first for Charlie. Barbara had two kids from her first marriage which ended in a nasty divorce.

When Barbara and Charlie were married, they could not afford a house. They reluctantly moved into the first floor of a two family house, owned by Charlie's mother. Barbara understood how difficult it was for Audrey, Charlies' mother, to accept instant grandchildren. Audrey had other grandchildren, so Barbara worried about the comparisons Audrey might make, as well as Audrey's acceptance of her two kids as additional grandchildren.

Barbara worried about how difficult it would be for everyone, including her own two kids, when they were thrown into the mix. She wondered if her own kids would be worried about having instant cousins. There was a lot to think about and a lot to accept and accommodate in this union.

At first Barbara's kids found it difficult to accept Audrey as their grandparent, and they had trouble calling her grandma. It got easier with time.

Charlie's mother Audrey lived in the upstairs apartment. Audrey was kind and good-natured but domineering. She had complete control of her children during the years they were growing and handled all the children's dilemmas.

Barbara and Charlie had a volatile marriage. When a fight ensued, Charlie would inevitably coerce his mother into the argument. Audrey consistently supported Charlie. At times she attempted to offer a consideration of a compromise between the two, but her son would never listen.

Barbara admitted Charlie's mother disliked participating, but Charlie relentlessly managed to drag her into the disagreement. Charlie sensed his mother's reinforcement. Barbara lost the battle every time, and she suffered in silence during these quarrelsome episodes. Barbara continued to place more blame on Audrey which kept both women apart. Barbara was pregnant within the year and now was worried that Audrey would favor her biological child over her two step children. The couple continued saving, but now with three children to nurture and no cheaper place to go, they reluctantly stayed with Audrey.

The circumstances remained unchanged for a few years. When the step children were closer to becoming teenagers, Charlie and Barbara bought a dog. Audrey, under pressure, agreed to the decision. Her one provision was they keep the yard clean. The children neglected the yard, and Audrey complained. She was annoyed and did not appreciate a dog in the yard. A battle ensued between Audrey and her daughter-in-law. In a fit of anger, Audrey ordered Charlie and Barbara to leave the house along with their children.

Barbara was actually happy and relieved. Charlie was devastated, but Barbara searched and rented a charming condo. She experienced freedom for the first time. Charlie was disoriented in the unfamiliar accommodations. He was displeased with his mother and irritable with his wife.

Audrey had treated her step grandchildren no differently than her biological grandchildren right from the beginning. This definitely helped in mending the fences. Audrey came to love the kids, and Barbara began enjoying the attention Audrey gave to the kids. A short while later, Audrey and Barbara mended their bonds. Their relationship was not perfect, but they were striving to improve it and communicate.

Neither woman wanted to admit the husband or son's blame in the situation. Charlie enjoyed the power his mother's approval gave to him. Charlie never considered how difficult it was between his wife and mother. They all suffered some pain in this dilemma, but they also got through it and gained some powerful relationships worth having.

Discussion 7

"If we would just slow down enough to consider what's true and real and always try to understand the way other people feel and be less quick to anger and show appreciation more and love the people in our lives like we've never loved before. If we treat each other with respect and more often wear a smile, remembering that this special dash might only last a little while. So when your eulogy is being read with your life's actions to rehash would you be proud of the things they say about how you spent your dash?" - Linda Ellis, Mac Anderson

Barbara and Charlie should have obtained a place of their own as soon as it was possible. Although Audrey had no obligation to encourage her son's autonomy, occupying the same house with one's parents destabilizes the couple's relationship by sustaining constant tension. It is possible the parent may manipulate the adult child. It is also possible, as in this case, for the adult son to manipulate his mother.

It may be difficult to forego sanctuary, but when we renounce safety, we are rewarded with independence and a confidence in our own ability. The adult child should not fear venturing out on his own. One must forego refuge and discover self-reliance.

Audrey erred in participating in the arguments between Charlie and Barbara. It was not Audrey's place to support either side during a dispute. The disagreement was between Barbara and Charlie. Audrey's opinion was not relevant or necessary. Audrey should have had the courage to walk away from every dispute.

Barbara was in a compromising position, especially having young children to raise and worry about. It left Barbara's options limited. Barbara's precarious position was evident in the way she handled her anger. Barbara lashed out one minute then backed down the next. Charlie was secure with his mother's approval. Charlie's hesitation was in his fear of developing his own life. His mother influenced all of his undertakings. It is imperative Charlie accept his wife as an equal and respect their marriage. Charlie needs to recognize himself and his wife and children as a separate family from his childhood household. Fyodor Dostoyevsky believed there was trouble in the world when he stated, "Much unhappiness has come into the world because of bewilderment and things left unsaid."

On the other hand, Audrey was saving the couple a lot of money, yet she felt there was no appreciation. She was also at the mercy of her son. It really became important for Barbara and Audrey to understand each other's problems and pain. That would bring both women serenity. Rumi sought to find peace and compromise in the words, "Out beyond ideas of wrongdoing and right doing there is a field, I'll meet you there."

Barbara was suppressed by her insecurity, and she had no one to rely on. Her options were few. Finding the courage to confront Audrey with her sentiments was one of Barbara's challenges. Barbara had a right to voice her own opinions and be heard, but she didn't trust herself or her right to do it.

Audrey had a right to her own privacy and opinions and she also fretted over disappointing her son. She wanted to help the young couple, but questioned how much support she was actually giving. She stopped trusting herself.

Our vulnerabilities can keep us at a standstill. Confronting them is an important first step in overcoming them. Many of us must find our self-esteem to stop our roller coaster ride with defensive and offensive behaviors. Our brightest glory and victory comes from within.

Reflections for Mothers-in-Law

- If you can't empathize, it is better to say nothing.//
- Support your son and daughter-in-law's dreams; dreams are necessary to life.
- It isn't easy to overcome fear. You need strength to overcome the fear of moving in another direction.
- Negative remarks are destructive. Keep your words positive and constructive.
- Don't tear things down when you have nothing to rebuild. It is easy to destroy something but harder to rebuild it.

Questions for Mothers-in-Law

- Are you fair in your treatment of your biological and step grandchildren?
- Do you make quick judgments about your daughter-in-law and her reasons for doing things without having all of the facts?
- Are you inflexible when plans change?
- Are you honest with your daughter-in-law by expressing how you feel emotionally?
- Do any of your behaviors cause you guilt or give your daughter-in-law reason to doubt you?
- Do your daughter-in-law's remarks or behaviors provoke you to speak in a nasty way?
- Are you critical of your daughter-in law's decisions?
- Have you ever looked for the good in people rather than searching for the faults?

Chapter 8 – Courage to Compromise

"He who cannot forgive, breaks the bridge over which he himself must pass."
- George Herbert

Being judgmental of our daughters-in-law can manifest in alienating our daughters-in-law. It is crucial mothers-in-law refrain from articulating assessments of sons, daughters, sons-in-law, daughters-in-law, and grandchildren. The energy put into this merits the outcome.

One daughter-in-law may be cooking gourmet meals served on a fancy plate and tablecloth. Another daughter-in-law buys boxed or frozen meals served on paper plates. Those of us who are more private probably enjoy tranquil walks and time to enjoy a good book.

A pacifier can become a contention between mothers-in-law and daughters-in-law. It perhaps has been called a crutch by some and to others a relief. Some mothers-in-law as well as some daughters-in-law attest to the advantages of the binkies. Many children suck their thumbs or suck on a pacifier. How soon a bottle or pacifier or thumb sucking is ended conveys the impression of an effective or inadequate mother.

A mother-in-law might be exceptionally tidy while her daughter-in-law might have an active social life, extending modest time to clean. How about mothers who devote time to volunteer work? It genuinely is up to those specific people to decide for themselves what roles succeed for them. At different times in our lives, we are ready to pursue a variety of tasks. As Confucius said, "To be wrong is nothing unless you continue to remember it."

If the baby is thriving and happy, it is irrelevant what one prefers. Scores of us believe we have more deficiencies than virtues, and perhaps this is why we assign our own aspirations on our children. When our children are flourishing, we feel victorious.

It isn't wise to impose our philosophies or make anybody be subjected to humiliation. On the contrary, differences should be honored but not exploit, offend, or diminish another human being in the process. There are people who are truly concerned with the latest research. It only becomes a problem when they cannot recognize or respect another's opinion. Every generation is sure they have all of the answers.

Mothers-in-law might be guilty of comparing children, and although unwise, it does not affect how much they love their sons. It is likely true to say a mother-in-law loves all of her children. They are all special in her eyes. She may make awkward remarks, but she does not mean any maliciousness in them or realize the implications. She may be attempting to be careful so her daughter-in-law isn't offended.

Mothers-in-law have spent years being able to freely say whatever they entertained without having these comments scrutinized. Now it is essential the mother-in-law watch what she says. Some might become more introverted due to the pressure. They do not want to have a problem erupt.

There are fluctuations and challenges that confront us every day. Some days we can pull more than our share of the load while other days we cannot even pull our own portion. If there is a competition, there will be a winner and a loser. The loser will walk away disgruntled and beaten. The loser may avoid contact with the winner. Sometimes we create our own competition. When a daughter-in-law shares the most recent event in her young child's life, it does not mean she is boastful. Pride can promote an arena of rivalry.

Forcing adult children into a competitive environment may cause anger, and frustration. Be mindful that all children can be depended upon to carry out distinct undertakings. Some children invite their parents for dinner, others are present when there is a difficulty, and still others will assume major responsibilities for their parents if the time and need arises. Love should not be built on necessity, guilt, or dependability.

Genuine love is unconditional and perpetual to all participants at all times. Because people think differently they respond in a variety of ways. Girls may call their mothers more often than boys call. This in no way constitutes the amount of love involved. Parents love their sons as much as they love their daughters. The love is demonstrated differently, but it is just as strong.

Story 8

"You have your way. I have my way. As for the right way, the correct way and the only way, it does not exist." - Friedrich Nietzsche

Sara was not overly excited about spending her vacation week with her mother-in-law Maggie. Sara hated all of the questions Maggie asked. Sara didn't lie to Maggie, but Maggie continually stared through Sara when Sara would answer. Sara decided to make the most of it for her husband Brian's sake.

Maggie immediately prepared food upon their arrival and then prompted Paul and Matt to eat all of it. Sara finished some food from both of her kid's plates. It was enough to satisfy Maggie's need to not waste food. Sara made excuses as she often did when Maggie put her in a tight position.

Sara passed the sippy cups to her sons and Maggie questioned when they would be using regular cups. It was the usual barrage and implied criticism, so Sara did not get too upset but simply stated, "when they are ready."

Maggie asked about their daycare facility and how many

hours they spent there each day. She was surprised at Sara's response of seven to eight hours. "I guess you don't get to see them much," Maggie said. Sara bit her tongue and responded, "We see them a lot and spend every minute with them when we are home with the kids."

There, she did it again, thought Sara to herself. I fall into her trap every time instead of ignoring her questions. Sara remained very quiet, and Maggie continued. "I guess Jen already has Luke toilet trained, and he can actually drink from a cup." Sara didn't want to sound sarcastic, but the words spilled out without reflection. "Well isn't that just perfect, like mother like daughter." That was when Sara was stunned at Maggie's reply. "Actually Sara, my boys were difficult in every way, and I didn't get them trained early on anything." Sara was speechless. She had assumed that Maggie was always looking for ways to be critical, and here she was admitting her flaws with child rearing. Sara would never have conceived Maggie was lacking in any way. Maggie was not less of a person just because her kid's toilet trained late.

Sara replied, "It doesn't really make a difference when they are trained. All of them get fed and toilet trained in time so who's counting?" Maggie smiled and stated, "I was not as calm with the kids as you are. You appear to be a lot more relaxed than I ever was. You are doing a great job, Sara." Now Sara was truly shocked and lamented her harsh criticism of Maggie to her friend Jenny. What she had assumed with all of Maggie's questions and interest was so off base with the truth. Maggie apparently was trying to find out how bad of a parent she was in her own mind. The goals she had set were obviously never attained.

Sara recalled how many times she had gossiped about her mother-in-law and her insistence on perfection in child rearing practices. Sara silently moaned to herself because nothing could be further from reality. Maggie saw the simplicity with which Sara handles the children, and she knows she never experienced ease at raising her own children. She worried her son Brian was comparing her to his wife.

Sara realized her mother-in-law had never considered herself a perfect parent. Maggie's perfection was only in Sara's mind. Sara and Maggie were embarking on a new relationship and navigating towards calmer waters. The relaxed body muscles were obvious as both women sat back in relief.

Maggie's attitude appears to be unreasonable, but when one considers how people are constantly compared, it is no surprise that Maggie lost her confidence in child rearing. Brian may not have been taking into consideration anything at all about his mother's child-rearing practices. It most likely was fabricated in Maggie's own mind about looking dreadful in her son's eyes. She was not as deficient as she believed. Countless women critique themselves harsher than they would assess an enemy.

The studies and conversations suggest this story is played out in a multitude of ways and settings. Perhaps if we were not all trying to prove our worth by being the best at everything, we would not be so fearful of failure. The rivalry will continue until either woman decides it is pointless to assess each other, and they throw down the gauntlet. There are times when comparisons are not being made, but people are sensitive when measurement is taking place. Honesty and openness lead to deeper sincerity in living.

"While on a walk one day I was surprised to see a man hoeing his garden, while sitting in his chair. What laziness! I thought. But suddenly I saw leaning against his chair, a pair of crutches. The man was at work despite his handicap. The lessons I learned about snap judgments that day have stayed with me for years now. The crosses people bear are seldom in plain sight." -
Annette Ashe

Discussion 8

"Out of suffering have emerged the strongest souls. The most massive characters are seared with scars." - E. H. Chapin

    Sara was in a precarious position. Sara and Maggie had different child-rearing practices and Maggie had a problem dealing with this fact. Maggie was insecure. She was nervous around Sara, and she believed Sara was being critical of her competence because Sara never took her advice. This of course was not the truth, but Maggie considered it to be the truth. No one was evaluating Maggie. She obviously did a decent job with Brian, and Sara thought he was perfect.

    Although Sara did not set-up this competition, she might have deflated it to some degree. Sara could have attempted to be more compassionate with Maggie. She might have asked her advice out of courtesy so the woman would be comfortable in her position, but she never thought Maggie was insecure. Sara had some dark moments, but she never shared them with Maggie. A bit of openness may develop the relationship.

"It does not matter how long you are spending on the earth, how much money you have gathered or how much attention you have received. It is the amount of positive vibration you have radiated in life that matters." - Amit Ray

Reflections for Mothers-in-Law

- Try to refrain from comparing yourself to your daughter-in-law.

- We all need more compliments than we do critics.

- Overlook flaws and focus on attributes.

- Keep in mind that altruistic attributes are priceless but many times go unnoticed.

- Recall the days you were an insecure new bride and mother.

- Understand you are the parent in the in-law relationship. You treaded the path so now avoid the pot holes.

- Don't ever be afraid to show your vulnerability to your daughter-in-law. You will not be demeaned, but you will become more human to her, which helps the relationship.

Questions for Mothers-in-Law

- Do you like to prove your efficiency and worth by criticizing your daughter-in-law?

- Are you always making comments about what your daughter-in-law is doing?

- Are you confused about the vibes you receive from the daughter-in-law?

- Have you ever believed your daughter-in-law is doing something better than you?

- Do you criticize your daughter-in-law in front of her husband or embarrass her on purpose?

- You and my son are couch potatoes. It's too bad you don't exercise more like Greg and Jenny. Do you like to work out?

Chapter 9 – Tolerate Failures and Changes

"You may give them your love but not your thoughts, for they have their own thoughts. You may house their bodies but not their souls, for their souls dwell in the house of tomorrow, which you cannot visit, not even in your dreams. You may strive to be like them, but seek not to make them like you. For life goes not backward nor tarries with yesterday. You are the bows from which your children as living arrows are sent forth. The archer sees the make upon the path of the infinite, and He bends you with His might that His arrows may go swift and far. Let your bending in the archer's hand be for gladness. For even as He loves the arrow that flies, so He also loves the bow that is stable." -
Khalil Gibran

Interference causes conflict between a mother-in-law and daughter-in-law. Most people do not like unsolicited advice. They request advice from others who are quick to agree. When they say they are searching for another viewpoint, they are really scanning for confirmation of their own perspective.

If a son takes his mother's advice and things work out, I would suggest the mother downplay it. Mothers-in-law must learn how to gracefully impart their knowledge and leadership without notice. A daughter-in-law might feel threatened if her mother-in-law is consistently getting involved. The mother-in-law may believe her daughter-in-law is young and inexperienced. Even if her advice is excellent, it may be unwanted. A couple wants to acquire answers for themselves.

A mother-in-law has to realize that what worked for her may not work for her son and daughter-in-law. Mothers-in-law may think that by pointing out the faults, they have helped. Your son will think less of you. If you demand too much of your daughter-in-law, you will push her and your son away. When a relaxed attitude is portrayed, your daughter-in-law's fears are lightened. The son will be upset if his mother continually upsets his wife. Being too involved will also make you appear to be a challenge. Your daughter-in-law will devise her own beliefs about you, and they may not be positive.

A good rule to keep is to remain silent. Allow the couple to allocate household chores. None of the mother-in-law's advice should be considered. Maybe your daughter-in-law's job is more stressful, or if your son gets home first, he starts dinner. If your son is happy and content, it is best to remain silent.

There is a fine line between guiding a child and acting out the parent-child relationship. It must be understood that they are adults. If a person is consulted on one subject, that does not give us the authority to voice an opinion on every matter. Having the permission to keep offering opinions has not been granted. Catherine the Great once said, "The more a man knows, the more he forgives."

Some people believe they have the hardest life, the most difficult circumstances to endure, and the saddest story to tell. They can win because nobody wants their problems. The majority of people keep their complaints about others under wraps. The truth is everyone attempts to tolerate each other. People do not enjoy being insulted, and they hang on to their pride.

Most people exaggerate good fortune and suffering. While some exaggerate, others pretend they are invincible. In the end, the conclusion is clear. Defenselessness appears when the sorrows of life happen. There seems to be no need to bring anyone to the breaking point. The façade crumbles for the daughter-in-law when she displays the insecurity she feels around her mother-in-law. She attempts showing pride, but ends up crushed when the mother-in-law jumps in and begins fixing people or situations appearing out of control. The husband is resented for not stepping in first. He lets his mother take over and the daughter-in-law is angry with herself.

The mother-in-law doesn't see the problem up close. She believes she is helping to make things easier. She is about supporting and has no idea of the issues or agenda that was planned. Her daughter-in-law seems to need help, and so she helps. The daughter-in-law is mulling over why she revealed so much of what was on her mind. That is what got her into the situation in the first place. The mother-in-law is feeling good about how she is handling things. The son stays in the background and at the moment feels good. He has no idea of the alternate plans each of the special women had arranged.

Lifting the blanket of impatience, we discover an actual person who has feelings, loves, desires, sufferings, pains, and opinions. Human nature should cause us to pause and reflect on that annoying mother-in-law, daughter-in-law, sibling, parent, friend, and even enemy.

To be human is to be weak, helpless, defenseless, and, at times, a failure. To become part of a humane style of living is the essence of true tolerance. No one wants to be the interfering mother-in-law or the arrogant daughter-in-law. The days of joking about the in-laws have ended because it hurts real people. The bumper sticker that says "CAUTION MOTHER-IN-LAW IN TRUNK" is finished. Respect is the new kind of bonding with the in-laws.

Story 9

"Opportunity... often it comes in the form of misfortune, or temporary defeat." - Napoleon Hill

Lilly and Ryan were married for five years. Lilly worked hard at her job as a computer analyst. It never gave her much time to be outside or get fresh air. Her husband Ryan suggested they go away for a weekend to a beach area. Lilly debated this offer. She really

Tolerate Failures and Changes

wanted to go, and she knew Ryan wanted to go, but they had been working so hard to save for a down payment on a house. After a difficult day, Lilly relented and agreed it was a great idea. They both needed and deserved the respite.

It was an impressive plan until Ryan's mother found out about it. She voiced her opinion against the trip, saying it would waste a lot of their hard earned money saved for the house. She eventually convinced her son Ryan it was frivolous to spend the money in this manner. She stated the weekend would pass by fast but having a house would be forever. Ryan went home to Lilly with his doubts.

Lilly was furious. She admitted it was a bit frivolous, but she sensed it was a mini vacation they both needed. She couldn't understand why Ryan had changed his mind. Ryan did admit he had discussed it with his mother Carol. Lilly was even angrier, and she blamed his mother for ruining their plans. After Ryan and Lilly discussed it and fought about it for hours, Ryan agreed to go, but Lilly, without warning, cancelled the whole vacation. The couple was now barely speaking to each other.

When Carol heard of the quarrel and the dashed plans for a mini vacation, she felt terrible. She began to honestly realize her interference could cause huge problems in the young couple's lives. She secretly wished her son had stood stronger in his own convictions to take the trip. Now she had to assume some of the blame, and she was very upset. It took a long time, but things did work out actually for the better because it was the catalyst for changes.

Discussion 9

Carol played a terrible role in this whole scenario. One must remember though that Carol is one person. She could not force the couple into doing anything. The guilt for Carol lay in the fact that she openly voiced an opinion to her son. Ryan is questioning if this idea was a good one or a bad one. He told his mother, and in the process, requested her opinion, which he never should have done. Ryan should have been more steadfast in his decision to take a vacation.

Lilly should have been more determined about going. Lilly could have told Carol how much she needed to get away and how important it was to her and Ryan. If her mother-in-law was not moved, Lilly could have stated she wanted to go and they were going.

Ryan and Lilly planned the trip weeks ago. Carol should not have ventured an opinion. How a couple chooses to spend their money is up to them. If they waste it, they face the consequences. If they save or throw it away, it is their business. Ryan should not have been so easily influenced by his mother. What a mother-in-law sees as essential and what a daughter-in-law and her husband see as vital can vary a great deal.

One couple I know sought to travel around the world and live in hostels or camp out in tents. They both quit their jobs and journeyed for one year. Both sets of parents thought they had lost their way. The couple came back home refreshed and renewed. They acquired good jobs, are part of mainstream society, and have wonderful stories to tell about their past adventures. Respecting everyone's freedom allows them to live their own dreams.

Tolerate Failures and Changes

Story 10

"We can't solve problems by using the same kind of thinking we used when we created them." - Albert Einstein

Doris had three sons and no daughters. All three of her sons were married. She was always worried when the holidays came around because she was never sure who might invite her and her husband Jim for dinner. Doris loved entertaining, but in recent years, her daughters-in-law wanted to make their own plans. The sadness arose when Doris was not included in their plans and wasn't invited anyplace. She began to feel she was just an afterthought, but she quickly pushed these negative opinions aside. She concentrated on what to cook for Christmas dinner for two.

Suddenly her middle son Andrew called and invited them to dinner. Doris was thrilled but nervous. Sharon, her daughter-in-law, was always cooking things Doris didn't like. She would say it was her family tradition. In Doris's mind, it was always her daughter-in-law's family traditions and never about her son Andrew's.

Doris was amazed how her son Andrew appeared to be gobbled up and absorbed into their family. Somehow Doris and her husband were left behind. Her son Andrew had discarded all of the traditions he had grown up with. When one entered their home, they would see pictures of Sharon's side of the family. None of Andrew's brothers were framed on any wall.

Doris made up her mind to bite her tongue and refrain from any negative remarks, not that she ever would speak negatively, but she would make an extra effort to taste the various dishes her daughter-in-law cooked. Doris was thrilled her daughter-in-law was kind enough to invite them.

Doris and Jim were quiet people as was their son Andrew. Sharon and her family were boisterous, and at times it was hard to tell if they were arguing or just enjoying a conversation. When the holiday arrived Doris and Jim approached the entrance to Andrew's home. Their son Andrew greeted his parents and escorted them to the den. Sharon called to Andrew for help in the kitchen. Doris' offers of help were declined, so Doris and Jim talked quietly to each other.

Upon the arrival of Sharon's family, which consisted of parents and three siblings, the room was bouncing with noise and laughter. Doris was hugged and kissed by all and then left alone to sit by herself. Doris and Jim and the rest of the guests were called to the dinner table within an hour. Everyone helped themselves and passed the plates around every which way. Doris got tired of asking what each dish was as it juggled by. Doris and Jim ate little, but no one seemed to notice. Drowned out by all the buzzing talk, Doris and Jim caught tidbits of conversations from various areas of the room.

As the day came to a close, Doris and Jim said their good-byes to Andrew and Sharon. Andrew kissed his mother saying "I hope you had a good time?" Doris smiled and nodded her head saying thank you to both. In the car, Doris leaned her head back on the car seat and closed her eyes. She didn't want to talk about the day, and she hoped Jim had enjoyed it more than she had.

Jim was quiet, and it was hard for Doris to read him. At the moment she was just too tired anyway. When they got home, there were messages of Merry Christmas from their other two sons. Unexpectedly tears gently streamed silently down Doris's face. Doris was confused, and she didn't understand why. She didn't even know how it happened, but she had completely lost all connections to her sons. It was as if she wasn't real to them anymore. Doris had no options. She stoically went to bed, but Jim and Doris stayed awake for a long time before finally being engulfed in a deep sleep.

Discussion 10

"Kindness is tenderness. Kindness is love, but perhaps greater than love...Kindness is good will. Kindness says, 'I want you to be happy."
- Randolph Ray

    Doris is most likely reminiscing too much about holidays of the past. Those days are gone and new memories need to be made. Doris is a gentle soul and doesn't like to create any scenes, but she really should make known her likes and dislikes to her daughters-in-law. She definitely needs to be more assertive. If she had taken control of a conversation it might have been beneficial to everyone. Doris and Jim might also think about having a shared Holiday after the holiday. This might give all of her sons a chance to attend and provide Doris and Jim a wonderful family visit with their sons.

    Doris would not feel so lost during a holiday gathering at her son's if she knew she would have the chance to experience her own holiday time later. Andrew and Sharon were kind to invite Doris and Jim, but they could have gone further and ensured both were comfortable. It is also the responsibility of Doris and Jim to engage themselves into the conversations. Sharing thoughts and ideas with others builds the first steps in bonds of friendship.

Reflections for Mothers-in-Law

- Offer little advice even when you are asked, and hold back on opinions and thoughts about how you did things.

- Staying neutral when your son and daughter-in-law are having a dispute is a sign of respect.

- Accept your daughter-in-law's personality type. Allow her to be herself.

- Tolerate the beliefs your daughter-in-law expresses in the presence of others, even if you do not agree with them.

- We are all different, yet we all enjoy family and love. Make the best at where you are and with whom you are spending the time.

- Stress is personal and should be respected. If your son and daughter-in-law need a reprieve, it is not necessary for you to approve but only for you to be receptive and silent about the decision.

Questions for Mothers-in-Law

- Do you communicate with your son only and neglect including your daughter-in-law?
- Are you offering opinions about how your son and daughter-in-law spend their time, money, or vacation?
- Do you watch your daughter-in-law to find fault and to correct her?
- Are you acting like a reporter with lots of questions when your son and daughter-in-law visit?
- Do you listen to your son complain about his wife after a recent argument and commiserate?
- Are you worrying about what your daughter-in-law might say behind your back?
- Are you looking for faults or talents?
- Do you want peace or war?
- Are you insecure or confident?

Chapter 10 - Children & Grandchildren

"The words with which a child's heart is poisoned, whether through malice or through ignorance, remain branded in his memory, and sooner or later they burn his soul." - Carlos Ruiz Zafon

All mothers can understand the highs and lows in marriage and raising a family. This should create a common bond between the mother-in-law and daughter-in-law, but this may also cause friction. A new baby creates upheaval when it arrives, and but it may also promote a peaceful, loving environment.

Many grandparents who are within a car's ride are solicited and anxious to baby-sit. Babysitting for grandchildren has its advantages and disadvantages. Although on the surface it might be appealing to spend so much time with the grandchildren, it can end up becoming a mine field for those grandparents who do not want to discipline the grandchildren.

Overstepping one's authority with one's grandchildren or complaining about one's grandchildren is but a few of the risks. There is a fine line between visiting and sitting for your grandchild. The same rules apply, but grandparents can be the enforcer or the too lenient grandparent.

They must not offer unsolicited advice nor ignore their daughter-in-law's instructions. This would be a huge mistake. They should know their place. When babysitting, a grandmother must abide by the rules set by the parents.

Children and Grandchildren

Considerations for the Mother-in-Law

"Kindness in words creates confidence. Kindness in thinking creates profoundness. Kindness in giving creates love." - Lao Tzu

Just because a mother-in-law has experienced motherhood and the rearing of children does not necessarily make her an expert. A mother-in-law should not assume her alleged expertise in the matter will be acknowledged by her daughter-in-law. A mother-in-law does not want to detract from her daughter-in-law's experience with optional advice. Unsolicited opinions foster disharmony, even when the advice is worthy. Caution should be heeded with solicited advice and kept within the boundaries of impartiality.

New ideas and experiments are on the market every day. The daughter-in-law may decide to take a chance on a new concept and sell a new product. The support the daughter-in-law receives enhances her confidence and lessens the friction between the two women.

When your daughter-in-law trusts you, she will confide in you and allow you to care for her child. Listening and following instructions promotes less antagonism. A mother-in-law does not want to become an adversary to the daughter-in-law. The daughter-in-law has the authority to set the rules for television time, bedtime, eating, snacking, and boundaries for safety. A mother-in-law who recognizes the authority of her daughter-in-law will bend to her daughter-in-law's requests even if she doesn't agree with the rules. This generates a relaxed atmosphere.

If one does not follow the orders set by her daughter-in-law, she runs the risk of not having access to her grandchildren. Trust and honesty is important in a mother-in-law/daughter-in-law relationship as it is in any association. A mother-in-law might ask for small courtesies and concessions which the daughter-in-law might grant. Communication and trust is solidified.

Criticism establishes low self-esteem and a lack of effort. When a child is judged, he is set for failure, and it robs him of confidence. Focus should be on the child's strengths. A daughter-in-law cherishes praise of her child, which stimulates greater achievement.

Comparisons result in uncertainty and mistrust of the person doing the contrasting. Competition hurts a child's self-esteem. Are the child's size, appearance, and ability important? Appraisals are subjective, distorted, and cause devastation to a child's pride. Diversity makes life more interesting. A mother-in-law should be careful of sharing information from one household to another. What transpires in one child's house should not be revealed and discussed in another child's house.

When step-children are added, life is confusing for everyone. Kids don't always want to listen to a step-parent, especially when they are teenagers. It is difficult to place our kids on the same level as our step kids. It is a high form of love. Not many of us reach that state, although we should all attempt to do it. The comparisons are further strained when we compare the biological and step children or grandchildren. It is best to abide by the standards constructed from the beginning. When anger develops, children must be dealt with fairly. If we keep the discipline and learning always tied in with love, we won't go wrong. It isn't so difficult to simply love others whether by blood or bonds.

Disciplining

"I Regard (Parenting) the hardest, the most complicated, anxiety ridden, sweat-and-blood producing job in the world. Succeeding requires the ultimate in patience, common sense, commitment, humor, tact, love, wisdom, awareness, and knowledge. At the same time, it holds the possibility, for the most rewarding, joyful experience of a lifetime, namely that of being success guides to a new and unique being." - Virginia Satir

As hard as parenting is, if we understand the requirements, we benefit along with the child. We are sending moral individuals into the world. By never being hit, perhaps they will never get physical with others. If we have used kind language and loved with a gentle heart, our kids will be empathetic and compassionate with others. Teaching kids how to control their temper, empowers them with real strength to accomplish great things. Overcoming unfairness teaches persistence. Teaching tolerance helps them accept others.

Although disciplining is the realm of the parents, a mother-in-law needs to have some authority to control any misconduct when babysitting. Disciplining is the daughter-in-law's domain. As was previously stated, small exceptions might be made for mothers-in-law who babysit.

A mother-in-law may discipline only with permission from the mother. If the grandmother is supervising the child for any length of time, she may be granted approval to instruct within the realm of reason. This is not suggesting allowing unruly kids to reign. Within limits and following the parents' guidelines, a comfortable system should be achievable.

The grandmother should be wary of inflicting her views and attitudes towards child rearing onto her grandchildren. She might have to compromise her convictions if they differ from her daughter-in-law's or a mother-in-law may see less of her grandchildren.

Story 11

"I am tired of people saying that poor character is the only reason people do wrong things. Actually, circumstances cause people to act a certain way. It's from those circumstances that a person's attitude is affected followed by weakening of character. Not the reverse. If we had no faults of our own, we should not take so much pleasure in noticing those in others and judging their lives as black or white, good or bad. We all live our lives in shades of gray." - Shannon L. Alder

Kara enjoyed the company of Amanda. Both women got along well together. Kara had a four-year-old son and a two-year-old son, and Amanda had a four-year-old son as well and a two-year-old daughter. Kara and Amanda were sisters-in-law, married to two brothers named Kevin and Dan.

There was only one problem in their relationship, and that was their mother-in-law Gail. She was kind and helpful, but Gail never ceased to upset Kara with her remarks.

Kara's four-year-old son Jim was of average height for his age but he was thin. Amanda's son Tim was about the same height but broader in the shoulders and heavier. Jim and Tim played well together, but Gail continuously commented on Tim's larger size. Gail equated size with ability and strength. Gail unconsciously interacted more with Tim because she was amused with his bulk. Jim was as strong or stronger, but being slight, he did not attract Gail's attention.

Kara tried to control her anger, but it was challenging. Jim and Tim were the same height, but when Gail would talk to a friend or another family member, she would always say Tim was taller. Gail would also mention Tim was going to be a big man. Gail never mentioned Jim.

Kara couldn't believe Gail's predictions. It amazed Kara,

Gail felt she had the right to even formulate them. Kara was defenseless. If she tried to say anything, it would be like sour grapes. Kara didn't care if Jim was shorter when he was grown. What bothered her was her mother-in-law's equating size with being better.

Discussion 11

"I am suggesting that as we go through life, we 'accentuate the positive.' I am asking that we look a little deeper for the good, that we still our voices of insult and sarcasm, that we more generously compliment and endorse virtue and effort." - Gordon B. Hinckley

Gail had a lot to consider. A number of issues may be learned the hard way. Pitting siblings or grandchildren against each other creates enemies and tension. When there is a winner, there must be a loser.

It is questionable how neutral Kara actually is. Kara professes being tall or short or strong or stronger is unimportant, yet she constantly focuses on every comparison made by her mother-in-law. If Kara chose to have faith in her beliefs, she might not be so bothered. She might even end the silly remarks with humor such as, "well it is a good thing they are not giving out awards for strength because I suppose Jim would get nothing."

It is possible her mother-in-law is not even aware of what she is creating. She may even be surprised if she found out and was confronted in such a manner. This could lead her to a defense of her smaller grandchild and a compliment of one of his attributes. When there is no understanding, which often happens, people hurt others unintentionally.

Gail is unwittingly causing a rift between her two daughters-in-law. They have a nice relationship, and it is in jeopardy. If Kara has enough aggravation, she will stay away from Amanda and Gail.

This would be sad for all of them. If the mother-in-law is using this as a control factor, it is even worse. Losing contact with grandchildren due to unkindness or irresponsibility is a shame.

Story 12

"Love is strengthened by working through conflicts together." - Anonymous

Paul and Babette had two children, Jeremy, who was five, and Kelly, who was seven. Babette prized herself with knowledge about the latest modes of child rearing practices. Emphasis was placed on reading to your child, so this is what Babette did every night. Babette's children were involved in a variety of activities. Babette desired to keep their minds and bodies active.

Babette's mother-in-law, Cheri, frowned on all of this. She believed in instinct and one's natural ability to care for their children. Cheri would make comments about Jeremy's manners or Kelly's constant interruptions. Babette was disposed to be defensive.

When Cheri was watching the children for Babette one day, she received the usual instructions upon the children's arrival. The children were to have no candy or desserts. They were to watch no television. Cheri was agitated but said nothing. She contemplated how to circumvent Babette's stipulations.

Cheri had not been well, and she had planned on presenting a movie for her grandchildren. Cheri yearned to see her grandchildren and did not want to mention her infirmities. She feared Babette would not allow the children to stay. Babette's last words were no television. Cheri did not fancy playing any board games with them because she had a horrific headache from her sinuses.

Cheri called her friend Lilly, who invited Cheri and the children to come over right away. Lilly loved to see Jeremy and Kelly.

Children & Grandchildren

Lilly immediately offered them two chocolate chip cookies. Lilly then proceeded to make the children an ice cream cone. With wide grins, the children finished the ice creams in record time. Shortly after, Cheri brought the children back to her own house and waited for Babette's return.

The children never mentioned the cookies or the ice cream. While preparing the children for bed, Babette helped Jeremy out of his shirt. Babette noticed brown spots on Jeremy's shirt. Jeremy confessed to the cookies and ice cream. When Cheri was questioned by Babette, she disparaged the visit as inconsequential. Babette was aware of the distance to Lilly's house and the necessity of a car ride and the use of seat belts. She also knew Cheri lacked respect for seat belts.

Babette retreated with her children for home. She declined Cheri's offer for tea or coffee. Cheri rolled her eyes. Cheri wondered how long it would take Babette to recover from this incident. Cheri shrugged. She reasoned when Babette needed a baby sitter, she would be called again.

"This we can all bear witness to, living as we do plagued by unrelenting anxiety. It becomes more and more imperative that the life of the spirit be avowed as the only firm basis upon which to establish happiness and peace." - Dalai Lama

Discussion 12

There are a multitude of challenges in this situation. We might all agree seat belts are essential. The consumption of cookies and ice cream is arguable. Cheri created a lot of problems for herself unnecessarily. She lost Babette's trust with just cause; Cheri casually violated Babette's criterion and authority. Babette might find it difficult to trust Cheri again. It was not Cheri's option to obey or disobey, and she jeopardized the children's safety.

Some of Babette's orders are debatable, but not the safety issue. Cheri is never granted any allowances to coddle her grandchildren. Because she has no clout, Cheri resourcefully circumvents Babette's authority. This is detrimental to the children and the mother-in-law and daughter-in-law relationship. A daughter-in-law who is perhaps strict encourages others, including her mother-in-law, to resort to innovative ways to pamper the children.

It is impractical for Babette to assume Cheri must give individual attention to the grandchildren all of the time. Jeremy and Kelly received constant attention from their parents and grandparents. They would have had no problem and might have relished amusing themselves. The parents had all of their many activities planned for them. As a result, Cheri felt compelled to entertain the children when they were visiting, but she was never sure how to pursue this endeavor. If Babette gives ideas to Cheri or choices in activities, it might help.

Cheri needs to improve her actions and earn Babette's trust and confidence by following her rules. Babette can loosen some of the unessential restrictions she places on Cheri once Cheri earns her trust. This could foster an exchange of ideas.

We all hold our own paradigms to be true. Mutual discussions might pave the way to compromise. It is still the parent's decision, and Cheri needs to ask for forgiveness, especially for placing the kids in danger.

Reflections for Mothers-in-Law

- Create bonds by focusing on what you have in common.
- Recognize the power of love in the grandparent child relationship.
- Attempt to listen to your daughter-in-law when she is discussing the children. Follow her guidelines.
- Heed your daughter-in-law's rules for her children and obey them, even if you don't agree.
- Accord your daughter-in-law space.
- React positively to your grandchildren's accomplishments of all kinds and on all levels.
- Extend equal acceptance of all your grandchildren, and never compare them.
- Refrain from fostering any competition between grandchildren.
- Friendships are ruined with comparisons. When competition is absent, jealousy is released.

Questions for Mothers-in-Law

- Do you deliberately break your daughter-in-law's rules or sabotage her restrictions and then wonder why your daughter-in-law does not trust you?
- Do you laugh at your daughter-in-law's fears or make fun of her about them?
- Are you praising the mindfulness and compassion in your grandchildren as much as their athletic or academic abilities?
- Who decides what an awesome attribute is?

Acknowledgements

I give a big thank you to my husband for his expertise in computer skills. Thanks to all of the women who took the time for an interview and survey, to those who submitted their names to my book, and to those who interviewed and surveyed but declined having their names mentioned. There are numerous other women who discussed their situations with me. All their thoughts and experiences helped in finalizing the results within the book.

I hope all will be inspired and encouraged to have healthy family bonds.

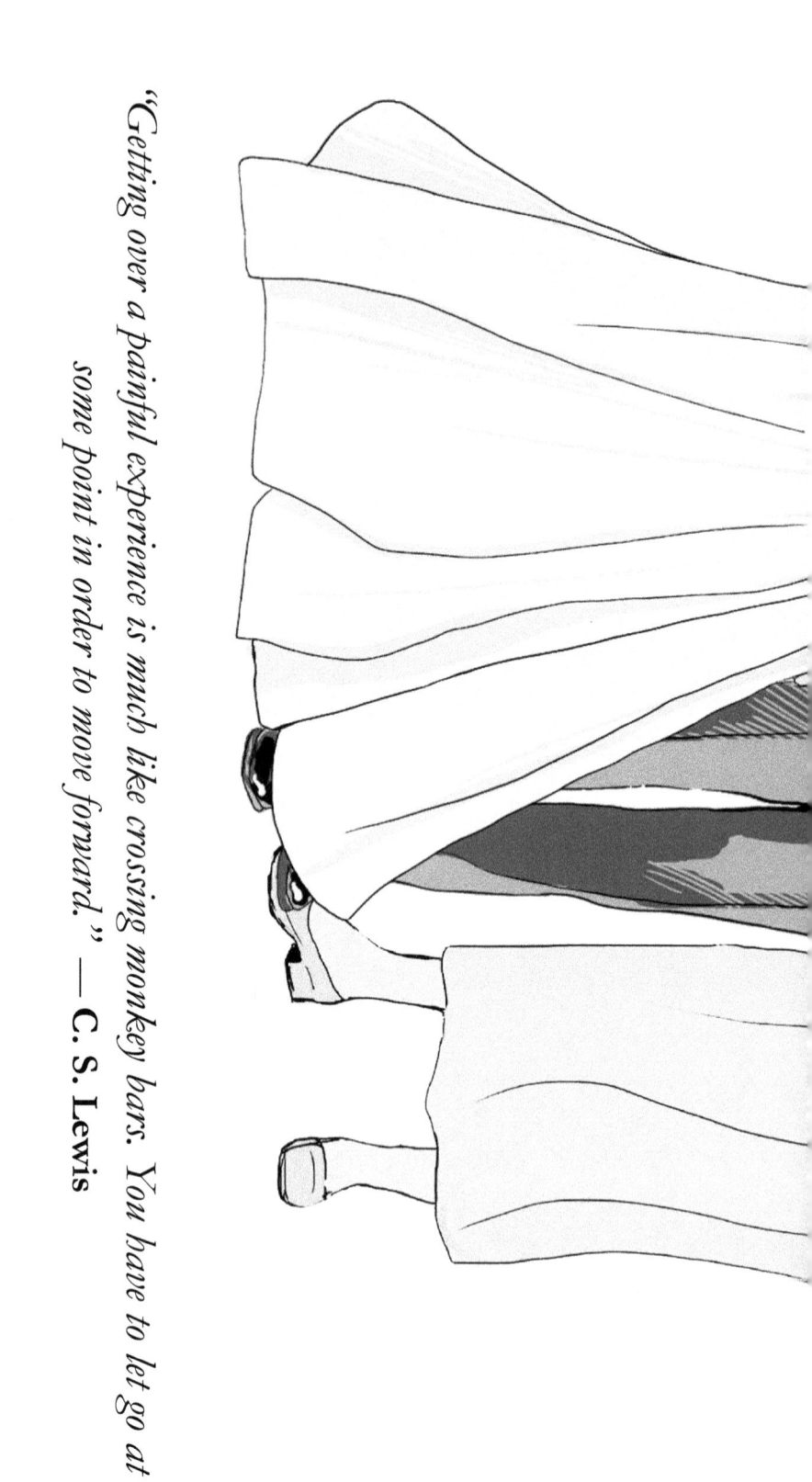

"Getting over a painful experience is much like crossing monkey bars. You have to let go at some point in order to move forward." — **C. S. Lewis**

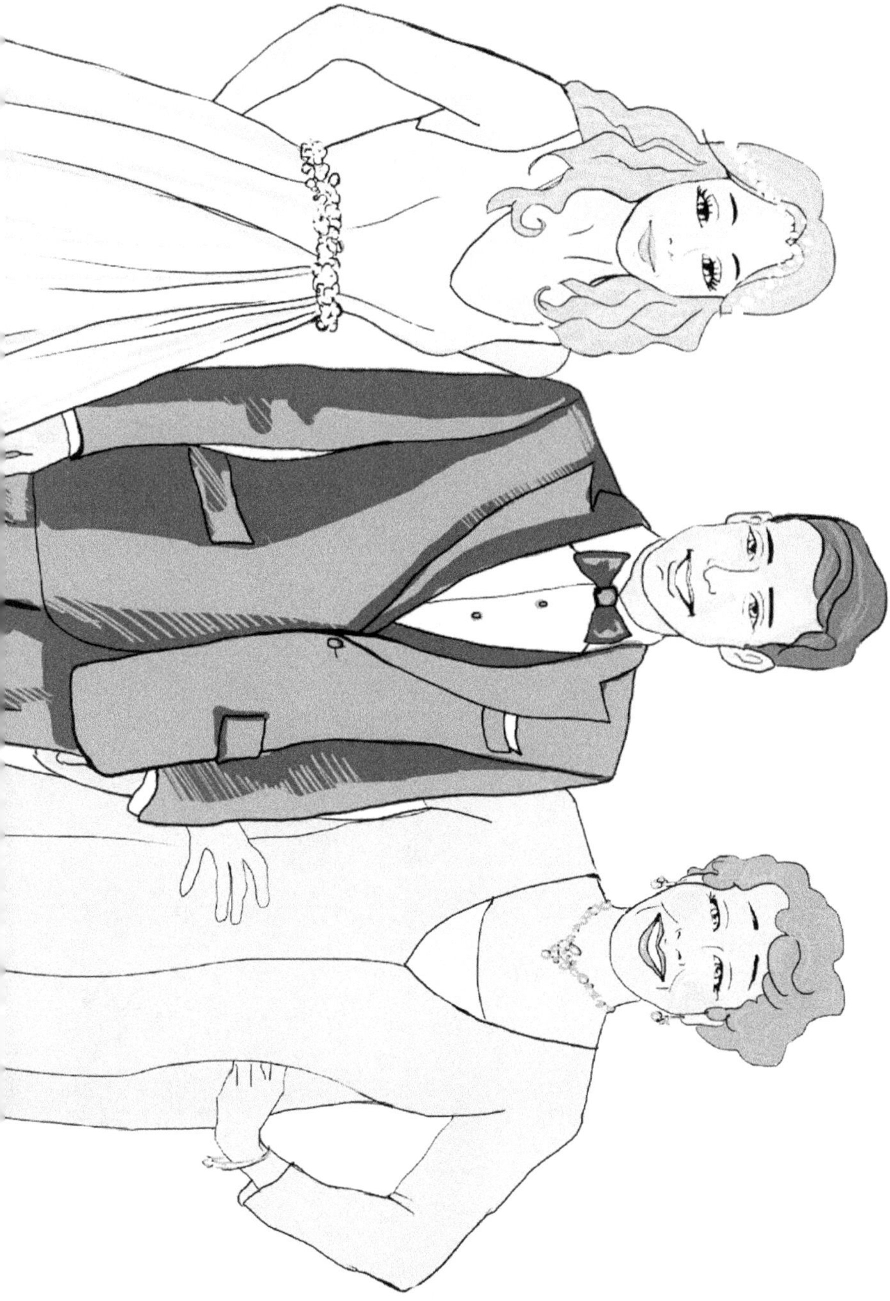

Questions for Daughters-in-Law

- Do you fault your in-law for putting the child to bed too late?

- Does your mother-in-law have some latitude pertaining to decisions for her grandchild, such as offering a cookie?

- Is she allowed some space when baby-sitting?

- Do you trust your mother-in-law to baby-sit?

- Do you make your child's restrictions difficult for your mother-in-law to follow?

- Do you look for problems in the way your mother-in-law interacts with the kids?

Reflections for Daughters-in-Law

- Your husband is under pressure when you are expecting a baby.
- Tolerate your mother-in-law's indulgence of her grandchildren as you do others.
- Allow your mother-in-law to visit with the grandchildren. These ties are special.
- Refrain from giving too many directions, and allow your mother-in-law space.
- Confrontations should not occur in front of the children.
- Toddlers fall on your watch, have mercy.
- Never foster competition between your children.
- Recognize the power of love in the grandparent, child relationship.

It is reasonable to assume Marie's controlling attitude toward Sean is causing friction with her grandson and daughter-in-law. She is possibly scolding Sean so much Sean is not going to relish excursions to his grandmother's. Most likely, Marie will never teach Sean anything by her constant disapproval and negative feedback. Marie's reprimands to Sean perhaps should be administered sparingly. If Marie feels Sean's behavior necessitates reproach, she might proceed affectionately.

It is possible for Katy to work with Marie to gain the desired results. Marie might have given her mother-in-law the option of allowing Sean to finish half of his dinner and then get the cake before she ploughed over the event. This would have put everyone on the same compromising page. It is important for Sean to view his mother and grandmother with love and a unified front. Each woman deserves some notion of power and control over their life.

The importance of compromise and collaboration needs reiteration. Those mothers-in-law and daughters-in-law who desire a workable solution might attempt teamwork. The unimportance of winning a small battle versus losing the war cannot be overstated. Never put the kids in the middle. They lose whenever there is division. Dividing up anything makes it less powerful. When people pull together they are stronger.

"Anger makes you smaller while forgiveness forces you to grow beyond what you were." - Cherie Carter-Scott

Children & Grandchildren

any authority in her own home. She would like to be able to indulge her grandchild with the piece of cake, even if he needed to take it home. Marie would feel she taught the lesson of not wasting food. She wanted Sean to be able to enjoy his cake because she made it for him.

Katy has not challenged her mother-in-law outright nor has she discussed it with her husband. Katy releases her rage through passive aggression. She undermines her mother-in-law on purpose and sabotages her mother-in-law's authority. She is relentlessly confounding the woman and diminishing the grandchild, grandparent bond. A Chinese proverb said it completely, "Anger is always more harmful than the insult that caused it."

Marie is weighed down under the subversion. She attempts to assemble a delectable meal, hoping to please her son, grandson, and daughter-in-law. She senses her daughter-in-law's disapproval as soon as Katy walks in the door. Marie can tell Katy is anxious to leave every time she looks at her watch. Katy doesn't even hide her desire to go. No matter how hard Marie tries, it never ends up being a happy time. She's out of ideas and ready to throw in the towel. It's becoming too much work, and frustration, and it offers nothing good in return.

Marie succeeds in pleasing no one. She loves her grandson and tries to model good manners, but this is not her role. Katy disapproves of Marie's aggressive interference because she finds it challenging. By doing so, Katy is teaching her son how to be disrespectful and ungrateful. If Katy does not attempt to correct Sean's insolence to his grandmother, she will unwittingly destroy Sean's bond with his grandmother. It appears Sean has already manifested skill at disregarding his grandmother's wishes. Sean is aware of exploiting adults for the things he wants. Katy does not comprehend the possibility that Marie loves or cares for Sean. Katy is most often enmeshed in the bickering criticisms. She has tunnel vision and goes to Marie's prepared for battle. Sean, as a result, is being deprived of his grandmother's love and positive attention.

Averting Andy, she glanced out of the passenger's window until they pulled into their driveway. Another burdensome visit with the in-laws, Katy concluded. An anonymous person once said, "People have to pretend you're a bad person so they don't feel guilty about the things they did to you. God forbid they be held accountable for their own bad deeds or thoughts. But Faith is seeing light with your heart when all your eyes see is darkness."

Discussion 11

"Anger is never without a reason but seldom a good one." - Ben Franklin

Hostility and control are bursting at the seams. Respect is missing all around. Sean is not the only one displaying fury. It seems many of the adults lack composure and tranquility. In this situation, Sean is the focal point of the dispute. His mother and grandmother are struggling to impose their own theories and practices. Sean is the one who is being manipulated. Sean would be influenced to a greater degree, if the women worked together and provided space for each other.

Andy, Sean's father, is on the fringe of the discord and not aware of the extent of the dispute. He is perhaps full of frustration and annoyance and directs it at Sean, a little boy in need of guidance, love, good role models, and rules. Sean is also aware of the frustrations and is taking advantage of the friction between his mother and grandmother.

The mother-in-law and daughter-in-law require an interpretation of their feelings and viewpoints. Neither woman is considering the others' feelings. The confrontations are escalating, and Katy is encountering relentless agony when visiting her mother-in-law. Marie, on the other hand, is experiencing the same anxieties on top of the workload involved with the meal. Marie feels unable to assert

he had already cleaned them. The battle ensued.

Katy intercepted, by scooping Sean into her arms. She hugged him till he giggled. Marie watched, resentful of this uncorrected insolence towards her. Sean was laughing and his anger was gone. Marie projected an angry look at Katy but again remained silent. Katy sent Sean to the bathroom to wash for dinner while Katy avoided Marie's eyes, dreading the consequences of her actions.

Sean was uninterested in eating his food. He opted to spread his vegetables around his plate. Marie always emphasized the importance of an empty dish. Tonight was no exception. Marie reiterated there would be no dessert if dinner was not finished, but Marie had already wrapped a large piece of cake for Sean to take home. Marie did not care if you were five or ninety-five. You were supposed to have an empty bowl. Marie began removing the dishes from the table. She did not pick up Sean's plate. When the table was wiped, Marie produced a chocolate cake. Sean asked for a piece. Repeating her original terms, Marie stated he could have some when he completed some of his supper.

Sean complained, but Katy whispered in his ear. He stopped eating and put his fork down. Katy requested a slice of cake. She consumed a small portion of the dessert. Katy gave the remaining piece of cake to Sean. "Thanks mom," Sean said as he devoured the cake. Marie said nothing. Instead, she loudly slid her chair backwards and hastened to the kitchen. Marie had spent a long time making that cake for Sean, her grandson. Tears welled up in her eyes.

Marie clanged the dirty dishes together on top of the counter. She declined Katy's offer of help. A short while later, Katy stated she had a headache, and would be going home. Katy's goodbyes were curt. Marie did not encourage them to stay. Andy was displeased with the abrupt departure. They rode home in silence.

Andy gripped the wheel, engrossed in driving. Katy sensed Andy's alienation. Sean complained he had to go to the bathroom. Andy abruptly retorted that Sean could wait. Katy was infuriated.

Story 11

"All kids are gifted some just open their packages earlier than others."

- *Michael Carr*

Katy dreaded the visits at her mother-in-law's house. Andy, her husband, was close to his mother. He never seemed to understand why Katy was nervous and anxious around her. Andy would just grin and say, "Ignore her."

Katy could not disregard Marie's remarks, especially when it involved their seven-year-old son Sean. During one encounter, Marie lectured Katy about Sean's temper. Katy's believed Sean needed time to mature. Hopefully, she thought, Sean would outgrow his petulance or learn to control it. Katy and Sean had not visited since that dreadful incident, and Katy wasn't looking forward to the inevitable clash.

Katy collected Sean and herself, and they climbed into the car and drove with Andy to Marie's house for dinner. The ride took about an hour. Katy was relieved she didn't live closer to Marie. While in the car, Katy gave Sean a long list of instructions regarding appropriate behavior. Sean kept nodding, and Katy sighed. In a short while they arrived at Marie's house. While Andy parked the car, Katy gestured one last reminder to Sean before proceeding up the walkway.

Marie kissed all of them at the front door and guided them into the den as she always did. When it was time to eat, Sean raced to a chair next to the dessert. As Sean dragged his finger across the cake a third time Marie requested Sean move to the end of the table. Sean frowned and banged his chair as he struggled out of it. Katy anticipated Marie's reaction, but Marie observed the commotion and said nothing. Observing Sean's dirty hands, Marie asked Sean to go to the sink and scrub his hands for dinner. Sean complained

Children & Grandchildren

Parents might limit the restrictions for their children so a grandparent doesn't feel like the warden. Grandparents should be able to administer some instructions. Trusting your mother-in-law to baby-sit assumes confidence in her supervisory skills.

If the children are at their grandparent's home, certain rules may be enforced that are not imposed at home. Or it might be the other way around. The criteria at grandma's house might be to; refrain from jumping on furniture, eating in any room other than the kitchen, helping one's self to food or banging on furniture with toys. It is practical in this baby-sitting situation for the daughter-in-law and the mother-in-law to be flexible.

Methods

You should respect your mother-in-law's old-fashioned approach to doing things. Every new advance on the market is not necessarily better, even if it is improved. Some understanding of past techniques will form a bridge of knowledge about a newer procedure. Familiarity breeds acceptance. Most of us are comfortable with what we are acquainted with. One-day today's methods will be regarded as obsolete. Remember, a mother-in-law can be taught a new way of doing things or instructed on a new device.

Compromising and integrating our assorted ideas promotes admirable models for our children and grandchildren to imitate. We can all follow our own path and get to the same destination.

A daughter-in-law who is too strict will inspire a mother-in-law to investigate ways too circumspect her authority. This is not in good standing, but and it could happen to the detriment of all. A daughter-in-law will not easily forgive a mother-in-law's deceit. This destroys the bonds of faith between the two women. If the mother-in-law defers to her daughter-in-law, then, as Willa Carter stated, "Where there is great love, there are always miracles."

A poor relationship between a daughter-in-law and her mother-in-law will damage the relationship between a grandmother and her grandchildren. To assume your children can have their relationship with their grandmother even if you have none with your mother-in-law will likely prove wrong in years to come. Maintaining the relationship between a mother-in-law and daughter-in-law is paramount to keeping the relationship between children and their grandmothers. Both women have obvious gains and losses depending on what they choose. Love is a principle concern, as Mother Teresa said, "Love is a fruit in season at all times, and within reach of every hand."

Appreciate Help

Sadly, it appears it is becoming obsolete to acknowledge kindness. Many people expect favors from others without gratitude. Unwittingly, we may refrain from accepting any obligations from these kindnesses.

We relish our accomplishments but refuse to recognize the aid given to us by others. We downgrade the huge assistance and influence of others. Grandparents guide and impress our precious children, and they often have profound effects. Grandparents deserve our praise for their undying time and effort. Likewise, many daughters-in-law come to the aid of their mothers-in-law in insurmountable ways. Recognizing these special angels in our lives is essential.

Chapter 10 - Children & Grandchildren

"The most important thing a father can do for his children is to love their mother." - Theodore M. Hesburgh

When a new baby is expected, there are many changes taking place. All involved need time to adjust. The new parents are about to learn the meaning of loyalty, love, sacrifice, and giving without receiving. Motherhood is universal. One thing is assured; things will never be the same for anybody involved. A daughter-in-law who is expecting her mother-in-law to be the daily care provider should relax and muster some appreciation for the time and effort which cannot be repaid. You need to acknowledge the fact that babysitting is not the same as visiting. If your mother-in-law is putting in effort, be grateful.

Likely your mother-in-law is in a situation where she will lose no matter what she chooses. If she complains, she risks making her daughter-in-law's assume she doesn't love her grandchildren or doesn't like to see them or babysit them. If she agrees to babysit daily, she might become exhausted and burnt out but afraid to complain. She may love to babysit for you every day, but giving up all her free time is a sacrifice of love. Appreciation would be welcomed and might even go a long way in mending any broken fences.

"Human beings are perhaps never more frightening than when they are convinced beyond doubt that they are right." - Laurens Van der Post

Some mothers-in-law are ready, willing, and able to take care of their grandchildren Grandmothers love their grandchildren, enjoy them, and want to see them. It would be hurtful for a daughter-in-law to use this as a tool of punishment against the grandmother if she should displease them in any way.

Questions for daughter-in-law

- Do you worry about what your mother-in-law might say behind your back?
- Do you invite your mother-in-law to visit at other times during the year?
- Do you include your mother-in-law in discussions or disregard her presence?
- Are you happy to listen to your husband complain about his mother and add a few complaints yourself without defending her in any way?
- Do you get angry with your mother-in-law's questions even when she is interested in a caring way?
- Do you ignore your mother-in-law when your friends are present?
- Do you stop to think and respect your mother-in-law's silence when you and your husband are fighting?

Reflections for Daughters-in-Law

- Respect your mother-in-law's efforts and feelings.

- Appreciate when she remains neutral during a dispute with your husband.

- Try not to assume you know the reasons behind peoples' actions.

- Insecurity breeds distrust and false notions. Attempt to trust more and judge less.

- Your mother-in-law did something good because you fell in love with her son.

Stan was happy and refreshed after a visit with his parents. It may ripple outward towards his wife and child sending positive affects their way. This empowers their home environment with positive energy. This situation may possibly be a winning situation if the daughter-in-law drops the control. There will be years for Stan to interact with his baby and he is present when he visits his parents. Power, control, and micromanaging might be the motives that cause us to consider some rivals. Getting over assumptions brings respite to everyone's life. Albert Einstein once said, "Not everything that counts can be counted and not everything that can be counted counts."

sults. Albert Camus encourages us to bend in his words of wisdom, "Blessed are the hearts that can bend, they shall never be broken."

Phyllis may have done a nobler service to both her son and daughter-in-law if she had invited both of them over with the baby. Mckenna was not getting the respite Stan was getting, which seemed to be most of the problem. Stan's time with Jenny was limited, and Mckenna sensed Stan should be taking care of Jenny. Phyllis was not aware of the fact she was interfering with Stan's fatherly obligations and slighting Mckenna. Phyllis was not allowing her son to be a father in Mckenna's eyes. He was relegating his duties to his mother.

Mckenna could have talked to Stan and requested he stay home more often and visit his mother once in a while rather than get everyone involved and upset. Mckenna could have tried to explain her point of view and then allowed Stan to have the break with his mother. Stan could have supported Mckenna at another time, thus giving her the break as well. Stan would likely be more apt to help her at another time because he was currently receiving help from his mother.

Phyllis and Mckenna should also have been able to talk things over and work something out. Phyllis might have made dinner "to go" for her daughter-in-law and possibly gained her respect and affection. Mothers-in-law can help and might offer to help, but they should not interfere or set patterns without the approval of both their son and daughter-in-law.

Sons must stand on their own feet. Daughters-in-law could recognize their husbands might need a break once in a while. Allowing a son to lean on his mother does not need to imply he is incapable. He might simply need and want a breather. He also may love his mother's affection for his child. At times daughters-in-law forget the husband enjoys his time with his own family and is proud to have his relatives involved in the care. The mother-in-law was thrilled to have her son and granddaughter visit. It was not work to her.

McKenna's reaction. She called my son immature and incapable of watching his daughter. She was so angry that Stan stopped coming. I don't know what my daughter-in-law was trying to prove, but she just made all of us unhappy. My son works full time, and he gets tired after a long day at work. I didn't mind watching Jenny. My daughter-in-law works part time because she goes to school. I just cannot figure it out.

"Now my son barely talks to me about anything. I know there are times when Mckenna needs to study, and she ventures over to her mother's house to let her mother watch the baby. Why can she have help from her mother but Stan can't have any help from his mother?"

I didn't have answers for Phyllis' plight. Perhaps in the mother-in-law, daughter-in-law relationship, there is a double standard, or maybe much goes unsaid. Perhaps insecurity or jealousy plays a role. It is hard to say why a mother-in-law appears to be such a threat.

Discussion 10

Each time something difficult and challenging has happened to me it has marked the beginning of a new era in my life." - Kimberly Kirberger

It was sad Phyllis could not perceive where she was going wrong even though she was acting decently. There are some daughters-in-law who would not be concerned by such an arrangement, but Phyllis and Mckenna had an interference problem.

Mckenna did not feel Phyllis was assisting her in any way. She alleged it was Stan's job to provide the care for his child. In Mckenna's eyes, he was shirking his responsibilities by requesting the help of his mother. If Stan had gone to his mother's once or twice, Mckenna probably wouldn't have been angry. This hurt Phyllis who meant well by her actions. She was saddened with the re-they can overcome their vulnerability and tolerate their faults, they might be able to put up with the faults they see in others. Being human permits us to receive and bestow kindness.

The Dalai Lama XIV said it best, "Every day, think as you wake up, today I am fortunate to be alive, I have a precious human life, I am not going to waste it. I am going to use all my energies to develop myself, to expand my heart out to others; to achieve enlightenment for the benefit of all beings. I am going to have kind thoughts towards others, I am not going to get angry or think badly about others. I am going to benefit others as much as I can."

Story 10

"Peace cannot be kept by force; it can only be achieved by understanding." -
Albert Einstein

Phyllis was a new grandmother. She was excited for her son and daughter-in-law but felt she was always doing the wrong thing. I questioned her further and she began her side of the story. "My daughter-in-law Mckenna, goes to school part time to finish her four-year degree. She only goes on Tuesdays. That's the night my son Stan is in charge of Jenny, their baby daughter. Stan leaves work early. When Mckenna first started school, Stan was nervous because Jenny would cry a lot. He began coming over to the house regularly, and to tell you the truth, I just loved seeing both of them. I would rock Jenny until she fell off to sleep, and then Scott, my husband, and I and Stan would sit down to a nice meal like we used to before Stan was married.

"I told Stan to come over every Tuesday so we could all eat supper. It went okay until Mckenna found out Stan and Jenny were coming. I must admit, I thought Mckenna knew about the arrangement, but apparently Stan never told her. I couldn't understand

night, and she let them put themselves to bed whenever they were tired. There were no rules, the only problem was she could never get a babysitter to watch her kids more than once. Regardless, she and her husband and children were extremely happy. She is now the proud grandmother of many grandchildren and is currently driving her daughters-in-law as crazy, in a nice way, as she caused her mother-in-law to be years ago.

One daughter-in-law has so many rules her mother-in-law is afraid to take any action without checking in with her first. In this situation, silence may alleviate many problems. In the circle of life, we will likely play both roles by being a daughter-in-law and a mother-in-law. If we comprehend this fact, we would put greater effort solving our issues and just getting along.

The complainers appear to never be content or pleased. For some people, others speak too slowly and don't finish quick enough to suit them. Some dislike vulnerability, openness, and gentleness. It is as if they distrust these virtues. Being outspoken scares some while being quiet unnerves others.

Most people believe strength is power and endurance. They don't think of quiet suffering as endurance. They almost dislike these people for not complaining, or they see them as weak. They tolerate races and people from different economic groups, yet they frown upon their own siblings who they believe are boastful. The question is, why is it easier to be tolerant of strangers but not of people close to us?

People don't perceive their annoying traits. It is good they cannot read each other's minds. They might behold a totally different picture of how others perceive them. Perhaps our pretenses should be removed and our defenselessness witnessed. Hurts, pains, and aches resonate with everyone. When we say we are all in the same boat, nothing could be more honest.

Most people hide fears. They wonder why they are nervous and stressed yet can't see the anxiety may be related to their fears. If

Chapter 9 – Tolerate Failures and Changes

"Any intelligent fool can make things bigger, more complex, and more violent. It takes a touch of genius and a lot of courage to move in the opposite direction." - Albert Einstein.

"Our greatest glory consists not in never falling but in rising every time we fall." - Oliver Goldsmith

If a son asks his mother for advice, it is likely going to be considered meddling by the daughter-in-law. She does not have the same faith and confidence in his mother, so she might resent any counsel offered. A daughter-in-law does not want to see her mother-in-law in a position of power. Following her advice is like granting her control, which is not what the daughter-in-law desires.

Accepting guidance never made anyone a fool. On the contrary, one should always trust their own judgment in the final analysis although, if we are confident, listening to someone's advice should not make us feel incompetent.

Tolerance might mean accepting a mother-in-law or a daughter-in-law who is dissimilar from us. They might have grown up in a different ethnic culture, economic status, or with a completely different set of rules. Whatever the case may be, the focus should be on the things we have in common. I recall what Henry Van Dyke said, "The best rose bush after all is not that which has the fewest thorns but that which bears the finest roses."

One daughter-in-law recalled how she drove her mother-in-law crazy with her lack of rules for her children. She was a free spirit and allowed her children to literally eat at any time of the day or

88

Questions for Daughters-in-Law

- Do you look down on all of your mother-in-law's ways of doing things?
- Do you consider your mother-in-law's ideas old fashioned and out of date?
- Do you make your mother-in-law feel inferior by pointing out her mistakes?
- Do you have a negative attitude about things your mother-in-law enjoys?
- Do you deliberately embarrass your mother-in-law in front of her son?
- Are you sabotaging every effort she makes to mend the relationship?
- Has she given up trying to defend herself because she believes she can't?

Reflections for Daughters-in-Law

- Try not to perceive every situation with your mother-in-law as a competition.

- Whether you win or lose a rivalry with your mother-in-law means nothing and damages the relationship.

- Holding your tongue is wise.

- Life is short. The regrets may come too late to change anything.

- Everyone likes to be complimented, and no one likes criticism.

- Your mother-in-law has more to lose emotionally than you do.

deficiencies. Olivia didn't understand Gina's arthritis. Gina's health wasn't discussed often because no one asked, and if they did, it was strictly out of courtesy, Gina believed, because no one ever let her finish before moving on to another topic. Gina got in the habit of stating everything was just fine.

When life finishes for any one of us, will we be happy for the ways we treated people? Regrets will be too late to change things. No relationships are trivial or games. Real people and honest suffering is part of the process. Perhaps questioning what it is we are trying to accomplish in all of this drama is the key to understanding, facing, and allaying our fears.

of them." Joe remarked. "Yeah Joe, but Caitlyn probably thinks I don't love her as much." Gina replied. "Look at it this way, Gina, if it wasn't this, it would've been something else." Gina shook her head. Neither she nor Joe slept that night. Gina's fingers were arthritic now, but she decided she would get her friend Louise to knit a sweater for Caitlin.

Discussion 9

"I realized that all the trouble I ever had about you came from some smallness or fear in me." - Mary Haskell

"All cruelty springs from weakness." - Seneca

Olivia expected her mom to indulge her more than she indulged her son's wife, yet she expected her mother-in-law to play fair. Gina had always tried to do this, but when the games and rules got switched up repeatedly, a person becomes predestined to lose. After reflecting, Gina remembered her fingers were becoming arthritic when Caitlin was born. She complained to her daughters, and they told her not to worry about knitting a sweater. They offered to give their mother's hand knitted sweaters to Olivia. Their daughters were too big for a lot of the sweaters. Gina was happy and thought everything was satisfactory. Now she understood it wasn't, and she could not retrieve the years.

Olivia alleged that Gina favored her daughters. She stated it countless times and even Gina's son Lucas accepted it as truth. Gina knew this was not accurate, but she was an amateur when dealing with her daughter-in-law Olivia.

All of Gina's efforts at trying to be a perfect mother-in-law that she could be backfired. The more arduous the attempts Gina made, the more Olivia wanted to establish her mother-in-law's

take notice of something Gina had done for one of her daughters. Gina was an expert at knitting. She knitted mittens and hats and scarves for all her grandchildren. All of them had received at least one sweater, at least, that's what Gina thought until one night. If given a request, she always tried to reply in the affirmative. Many times she just threw out offers to help. "If you need a babysitter," she would say, "I'm available."

Olivia, Gina noticed, was always friendly when the two of them were alone, but never when there were others around. Gina recalled times when Olivia was rude to her but talked to Gina like they were best buddies when all the company left. Olivia rarely called Gina, but Gina made excuses for her. She's probably busy, she would think.

Gina always brooded over how much Olivia liked her. It was as if Olivia resented her for not helping yet refused any offers of help Gina tossed out. As Gina got older, her daughter-in-law one day commented her youngest daughter Caitlin never got a hand knitted sweater from her grandmother. Gina felt horrible about this. She had in good conscience thought she had knitted sweaters for all of her grandchildren.

Gina couldn't forget the expression on her granddaughter's face when Olivia made the comment. Olivia felt justified with the whole matter and went on to state that "daughters are daughters and daughters-in- law are daughters-in- law." Olivia had a wide smile on her face, but it wasn't a happy smile. There were no crinkles at the corners of her eyes. Gina had prided herself in always being fair. Now she was beside herself with worry. Her husband tried to calm her down. He stated, "Gina, you worry about being nice to everyone, don't beat yourself up." The conversation didn't help. The tears streamed down Gina's face and sobs were uncontrollable. "I guess," she slobbered, "mothers-in- law make daughters-in-law mad but daughters-in-law make mothers-in- law sad."

Joe put his arms around Gina. He held her tightly. "I love you Gina, and I know you on the inside. You would never hurt any

If a daughter-in-law relates to her mother-in-law only by what she perceives from her husband's interaction with his mother, she will miss a lot of inside information. Her first thought is to render protection for her husband, when there is probably no need for such action. Playful verbal bantering between a mother and son is typical, but it can be misjudged.

Mothers-in-law may be completely unaware of the analysis their daughters-in-law are making. A mother-in-law may persist in being blunt in her behaviors because she understands her son appreciates her love for him. The doubt may possibly enter when the daughter-in-law interprets what her actions are implying. Rule of thumb, sons should do their own interpreting because they understand and love their own mothers.

Mothers-in-law and daughters-in-law who are cognizant of the bonds will not engage in this destructive manner. When your mother-in-law compliments another family member, you cannot interpret this as a format for a rivalry or a purposeful insult. When anyone is tired, they say stupid things, and Thomas Szasz said it pointedly, "A child becomes an adult when he realizes that he has a right not only to be right but also to be wrong."

Story 9

"What you dislike in another take care to correct in yourself." - Thomas Spratt

Olivia was married to Gina's son Lucas. Gina also had three grown daughters. Olivia and Lucas were raising three daughters of their own. Gina tried hard to keep please her daughter-in-law and her own three daughters. No small task, she laughed amongst friends. Her daughters often requested her help, and she was always willing to assist. Olivia never asked for help, but she would always

who have had mastectomies and have no choice to make.

Perhaps we must remember when our children reach the age of achieving success, we will not be the people they will be thanking for their success. At that period in time, they will most likely have a significant other who is supporting them and cheering for them. The circle of life plays out again as daughters-in-law convert to becoming the mothers-in-law who are possibly striving for a chance to spend time with their sons or grandchildren.

It is difficult for mothers-in-law to scarcely have time to interact with their sons. If a son chooses to remain silent, mothers need to respect that decision. His relationship with his wife is most important. The doubts must be put to rest. This is more difficult if a daughter-in-law proceeds to take advantage of this position and shuts her mother-in-law out of her husband's world. The big picture is hard to see, or the daughter-in-law simply may not want to observe it.

Most people turn out to be parents at some period in their lives, so it's unwise for one mother to deprive another mother of having a relationship with her child, even if that child is an adult. Even without rules, the competitiveness amongst the women would continue. The advice presented from both factions should be considered. J. Petit Senn says, "It requires less character to discover the fault of others than to tolerate them. Something to compliment and finding common ground can be found."

There is a distinctive threshold for pain, anxiety, and sensitivity. What serves for one child does not work for another. One child is easier to soothe than another. One child needs more of a sense of security than another. Everything isn't a competition.

When a mother-in-law speaks bluntly, her daughter-in-law can misinterpret the truth within the words. This can easily happen if a daughter-in-law chooses to interpret the mother-in-law's remarks in a negative manner. This is the closest thing to a disaster in the relationship because her mother-in-law loves her son unconditionally.

Chapter 8 – Courage to Compromise

"Some tension is good for the soul to grow, and we can put that intention to good use. We can look for every opportunity to give and receive love, to appreciate nature, to heal our wounds and the wounds of others, to forgive, and to serve." - *Joan Borysenko, from Handbook for the Soul*

Most people at one time or another contemplate their imperfections and their strengths. It is much simpler to perceive the failings of others rather than to see our own. Daughters-in-law need to stop assuming every insignificant remark spoken by their mothers-in-law was meant to be a rebuff to them. Instead of distancing this woman, they should get clarification.

Some of us enjoy cooking. Others tolerate it. Some keep an orderly house while some of us enjoy the lived in look. Many mothers are busy tending to children   bringing them to all kinds of activities and sports events. How we choose to spend free time is personal. Being involved in any associations might leave us little time to clean house or tend to other chores.

My discussions and observations suggest mothers-in-law and daughters-in-law dispute things such as the use of a binky or pacifier, toilet training, walking, speed of growth, and feeding techniques. As sure as a daughter-in-law does not want mother-in-law advice, so do friends and family not want someone else criticizing, them even if that person is correct in their thinking. None of the choices improves inner qualities of goodness. Criticism never operates in a supportive manner.

Another area of contention is bottle-feeding versus breast-feeding. There are countless pros and cons for both sides. The point is surely not which is better, but why mothers-in-law and daughters-in-law make it a competition. There are women out there

Questions for Daughters-in-Law

- Is it distressing when your mother-in-law declines a baby-sitting request?

- Do you formulate quick judgments about your mother-in-law?

- Are you uncooperative when your mother-in-law alters your proposals?

- During a quarrel between you and your husband, does your mother-in-law support her son or remain neutral?

- Are you provoked into clarifying your actions?

- Do contrary statements from your mother-in-law interfere with your thinking for an extended period of time?

- Are you intimidated about making a decision without another's confirmation?

Reflections for Daughters-in-Law

- Be cognizant of the vulnerability of others, including your mother-in-law.

- Learn from past mistakes of assumptions.

- Do not misunderstand the questions. Listen carefully.

- Admit your vulnerability and request help when in doubt.

- Be flexible and see both sides of an issue by compromising.

- Don't put your husband in the middle when dealing with your mother-in-law.

- When you have reservations, arrange for additional reflection time before acting.

- Never speak without thought.

The apprehension Mary exhibits originates in her uneasiness about sharing her children's love with other people. Her fears may be ungrounded, but they exist and require attention. Ignoring the problem does not allow one to escape it. Mary panics about what might be discussed in her absence. She withdraws in suspicion. Her children may perpetuate her apprehension.

Peg's rapport with the grandchildren is illusive. It could improve if Mary realized there was enough love to share. The more we share love; a greater amount comes back to us. Steve might attempt to bolster his own self-confidence with a request for space for himself. Peg's sentiments could have been expressed openly.

It is still possible for Peg and Mary to have a straightforward discussion. Peg merits a reprieve, and Mary warrants compassion amid surmounting stress. Peg deserves more than a fractured relationship with her grandchildren, and she attempted to change it. Peg might be able to confront her son and request help in dealing with this problem. It is likely Peg may have to challenge Mary and simply state her concerns. Mary has never confronted her own fears and may not even realize she has them. Kimberly Kirberger explained growth by commenting, "For me growth begins immediately after I am able to admit my mistakes and forgive myself."

Discussion 8

"Challenges make you discover things about yourself that you never really knew. They're what make the instrument stretch—what makes you go beyond the norm." - *Cicely Tyson*

The relationships are fractured. Mary's fearfulness has kept Peg from being close to her grandchildren. Trust is needed as well as communication. Peg struggles to retain a connection with her son and daughter-in-law. She loves her daughter-in-law and her grandchildren, so she accepts all conditions. This is commendable, but not a solution. Adopting a subordinate arrangement slights a healthy growth of actual love. The bonds exhibited by Mary and Peg are superficial. Honest connections of love and trust were never allowed to grow and flourish.

Deeper feelings may be rewarded with a sense of satisfaction. There are many places in our hearts for love to grow and develop sends. "Jealousy is the dragon which slays love under the pretense of keeping it alive." This quote was spoken by Havelock Ellis, and the insight in the statement is incredible.

Securing one tiny area in a grandchild's, son's daughter's, daughter-in-law's, or son-in-law's heart should be more than acceptable and worthy of the effort. The infinite joy and everlasting imprint left on the heart will be forever. If our children can't learn to love others and forge connections to other family members, they will not have any roots connecting them to any relatives when they are grown. This could come back to bite everyone, when there is nobody they care enough about to come back and see.

Having contacts with only one side of a family is a disadvantage. Children are deprived of all of the emotional and physical benefits that would have been of value to them. Parents need to ask themselves if what they are doing is beneficial to their child.

she said, "Fear is a disease that eats away at logic and makes man inhuman."

Peg's grandchildren were currently in college. They additionally were never allowed to visit their grandmother, without their mother's presence. Mary insisted on supervising the visits. This system cultivated a distant relationship for Peg and her grandchildren. Peg received obligatory telephone calls and visits, but the relationship was deficient. Peg's grandchildren acted on cue rather than on their own emotions, which almost appeared to be masked.

Spontaneity was gone, and the grandchildren were told where and when to say this or that. As the habit continued through adolescence and high school and college years, everyone got used to the manner, but Peg always felt deprived of a genuine emotion from her grandchildren. Now she never saw her grandchildren because they had moved away from their parents and visited infrequently. Peg thought they had learned their lessons well and never looked back. She shook her head and said, "Their own mother now suffers their loss."

"Confidence, like art, never comes from having all the answers; it comes from being open to all the questions." - *Earl Gray Stevens*

Peg recounted the time she sought to visit a grandchild at college. The University was close by. Peg extended a proposal for lunch. The young man seemed thrilled and accepted his grandmother's invitation. The day prior to the lunch date, Peg received a message from Mary. A profusion of excuses spewed from Mary about why the lunch date had to be cancelled. The young man had exams and it was an inopportune time she blurted. Mary stated she was relaying the message for her son due to his stressful agenda.

Peg sincerely noted and believed the proposal was declined because Mary uncovered the discreet overture. Peg relinquished in defeat.

Story 8

"To doubt everything or to believe everything are two equally convenient solutions; both dispense with the necessity of reflection."

- Jules Henri Poincare`

Mary glanced at her watch. She wanted to prepare some plans for her meeting in the morning. It was getting late. Mary's eyes cut across the room to where Steve was sitting. Mary demanded Steve get the car, stating it was time to leave. Peg shot a look at the clock on the wall. It was still early. Peg steamed at her daughter-in-law's usual early departure. Peg was agitated the way her daughter-in-law Mary dominated her son Steve. Just once, Peg wished Steve would speak for himself.

Steve had been married to Mary for over twenty years. In all of those years, Steve learned peace came with his submission. Steve noticed the disappointment in his mother's eyes, but he knew Mary must want to hurry home to do something she considered important.

Peg learned to accept Mary's authoritative bearing towards Steve. He acquiesced perpetually. Peg resigned herself to her son's subordinate situation. Mary never allowed Peg to enjoy some time alone with her son. Mary was consistently present whenever Steve and Peg were conversing. Peg was cautious and prudent about every word she spoke to Steve. Whenever Peg invited her son and his family to dinner, Mary responded for them all. Steve refrained from replying until he addressed the question to Mary. Peg laughed as she recalled one incident when she phoned her son at work and requested the family come to dinner. Her son expressed pleasure, and Peg was delighted. That evening, Peg received a call from Steve who defaulted on the engagement. Peg cried and shook her head as she recollected the event. Peg learned quickly to appeal to Mary first and foremost. Marian Anderson expressed the power of fear when

Strength in Challenges

"If you want something very, very badly, let it go free. If it comes back to you, it's yours forever. If it doesn't it was never yours to begin with."

-Anonymous

Sometimes mind games can become part of the scenario. It is difficult for an anxious person to be receptive. They might expect it will be used against them. They limit their own involvement and the participation of others. Their sensitivity incites distrust, and they view all people as competitors. Every person becomes a potential trickster and credibility is non-existent.

Love and support achieves the fulfillment of affection and good will. Changing our attitudes rather than attempting to alter the perspectives of others, may promote growth. Living with disagreements is possible.

Insecurity keeps a daughter-in-law fearful. Self-doubt will keep a mother-in-law silent. Lack of self-confidence will keep both a mother-in-law and a daughter-in-law from communicating, which renders the relationship meaningless and places the husband/son in the position of possibly becoming the constant intermediary.

Building self-confidence makes one able to overlook many thoughtless remarks. It affords the ability to ascend intentional or unintentional hurt.

guide. Likely this can leave us feeling stabilized, not undermined.

Apprehensive people most often presume others take advantage of them. In their anxiousness, they presume they are laboring intensely yet being taken advantage of. They are investigating work ethics as they strive to be noticed and admired. Daughters-in-law value the opinion of their husbands.

These appraisals made by the husband influence the value the woman places on her self-worth. This is not a positive thing for the woman to depend upon. Her husband's judgement bears little weight in the final analysis of who they are as a person. The mother and wife must appreciate their own importance based on their own judgments.

A husband's support of his wife encourages stability in the marriage, but one must be aware as Ann Benson mentioned, "Marriage goes in waves. You've got to be patient. People bail and give up on their marriages way too early. They just don't put the work and the effort into it. The ego gets crushed a lot of times, because that can be a big downfall." Having a strong in-law relationship actually strengthens a marriage.

Endless worrying about the reactions of others impedes a comfortable relationship between a mother-in-law and daughter-in-law. Another's motives can be problematic. A mother-in-law and daughter-in-law should not want to jeopardize their affection for each other by considering unsound information. People love to talk and causing friction can be exciting. It is similar to enjoying a mystery story, except these are real people and real people get hurt.

snubs to affect our ability and dignity. Insecurity breeds contempt for any kind of boastful comment. Our insecurity and competitive nature, keeps us at arm's length, away from each other. Viewing each other in a more vulnerable way just might help us to accept each other. Appreciate each person's effort to live their own life. In practicality, the lives of others do not necessarily revolve around our life.

Doubting ourselves causes us to be less humble in demeanor. Sensitivity will account for our concealment and embarrassment. This makes us act pretentious. Our frail egos analyze mistakes. A mother-in-law or daughter-in-law is obliged to prove she is capable. Anything less is failure, which threatens our self-esteem.

When our performance is inadequate, we are anxious about the harsh judgment of others, particularly our mother-in-law or daughter-in-law. This leads us to self-doubt. It is amazing the power one can wield over another without permission. It is astounding people can hurt each other so deeply without a care.

We may identify ourselves as inferior, yet we yearn to emerge outstanding. Even when the support of others is absent, our confidence can keep us whole. Words and actions produce turmoil and doubt how others perceive or trust in our ability. When we demonstrate confidence others have faith in our ability.

Fluidity of Status

"The greater the obstacle, the more glory we have in overcoming it". - Moliere

At times a daughter-in-law will not heed a mother-in-law's guidance because she fears her self-worth is in jeopardy. If we trust in our own potential, we can let go of control and let others be the

Chapter 7 – Overcome Fear

"You gain strength courage and confidence by every experience in which you really stop to look fear in the face." - Eleanor Roosevelt

Developing your self-worth enhances your self-esteem. Talents and abilities are unique to everyone. Ideas are considered throughout the day and are reviewed and changed constantly. It is ridiculous to assume we are the sole topic of another's thoughts. Confidence and faith in the relationships with other people divert any unwarranted, antagonistic feelings. Constant fear can paralyze us even though what we fear may not happen.

Changes are fearful whether they are good or bad. Life is about change, growth, and evolvement. Some of it is hard, but most of it is exciting as well as interesting. Acknowledging that everyone has changes places us on the same team. One team can appreciate the other team due to the common grounds and problems. The things we fear are not as scary when we get up close and attempt to understand them. It is kind of like our knowledge of people or the mother-in-law and the daughter-in-law.

Self-Doubt

"The greatest thing in family life is to take a hint when a hint is intended, and not to take a hint when a hint isn't intended." - Robert Frost

Confidence is important to our survival. If we have faith in our own knowledge, we are less likely to allow the daily defeats and

Questions for Daughters-in-Law

- Do you joke about anything pertaining to your mother-in-law?

- Do you consistently get the last word in if you have a discussion?

- Do you constantly see your mother-in-law's faults?

- Do you discuss personal things about your mother-in-law with others?

- Do you share a joke with your mother-in-law or is she the joke?

- Does it amuse you to embarrass her?

Reflections for Daughters-in-Law

- Tell your mother-in-law about lost sleep or a sick baby. She cannot read your mind or help you if you do not tell her.

- Give your mother-in-law space to show love and concern for her son. Consider the fact that she is his mother.

- Be thankful for dinner invitations, baby-sitting, and the listening ear.

- Honor your mother-in-law on Mother's Day.

- Treat your mother-in-law the way you would want your daughter-in-law to treat you one day.

- Don't accept things from your mother-in-law you do not want, just say no.

- Help out with dishes after a meal.

- Don't criticize, being right or wrong doesn't matter.

felt free to accept or reject. Cassie was not pressured by Nancy's recommendations.

Both women liked each other. They saw faults but overlooked them. Both women dwelled on the good things about the other person, and this made their relationship strong. They were not competing or comparing. They were decent and fair with each other. Most of all they were considerate.

Cassie deferred to her mother-in-law at times and Nancy deferred to her daughter-in-law. Cassie and Nancy's relationship would make many mothers-in-law and daughters-in-law envious, yet all of us are capable of such a relationship with a little work, effort and respect. An Anonymous person spoke inspiring words of wisdom, "God is always trying to give lessons to us but our minds are usually too full to receive them."

full green plants, she remarked how beautiful they were. Nancy then turned to her daughter-in-law and said, "You must have just bought them and replaced the other three." Cassie was shocked. She stared at her mother-in-law for a few seconds, and they both burst out laughing. For the rest of the visit, if either woman mentioned the plants, they had another laugh. Cassie spoke with love about Nancy. Cassie said how Nancy always went on vacation with them. Nancy would baby-sit while Cassie and Sean went out by themselves.

Cassie's amusing stories were inspiring. They proved that the mother-in-law and daughter-in-law could manage a compatible and loving relationship. They incorporated honesty, understanding, respect, and a dose of humor.

"Pride is spiritual cancer; it eats up the very possibility of love or contentment or even common sense." - C. Lewis

Discussion 7

"It is not good for all your wishes to be fulfilled; through sickness; you recognize the value of health, through evil; the value of good; through a hunger; satisfaction; through exertion, the value of rest."   From an old Greek book of wisdom

Cassie and Nancy clearly have a wonderful relationship. They enjoy each other's company. Cassie accepted and respected her mother-in-law.

Nancy was respectful of Cassie. She never mentioned the laundry. Nancy pretended not to see the laundry. She gave her son Sean and Cassie space and time. She blended into their lives without intruding. She did not try to influence their actions. Nancy never attempted to dictate instructions. She did offer advice, which Cassie

years, they lived a short distance from Nancy. Cassie recalled how busy she was when her children were younger than they were now. Cassie said how much she loved plants, but she admitted at times she forgot to water them. Her mother-in-law was a green thumb plant person. When her mother-in-law Nancy would stop by for a visit, she would pull out all of the brown dead leaves and water Cassie's plants. Nancy would then instruct Cassie on how to take better care of them.

If Nancy came unexpectedly and Cassie had piles of laundry all over the kitchen floor, Nancy just stepped over them and made her way to a chair without blinking an eye or losing a step. Nancy never mentioned the dirty laundry, and Cassie laughed as she remembered. Nancy would invite Cassie to lunch. Nancy always chose the restaurant, but she allowed Cassie to have veto power. Cassie recalled using her veto power only once. Nancy had chosen a fish restaurant, and Cassie hated fish. That particular time they chose a restaurant they both agreed on.

Cassie always had three plants hanging in the den by the window, as she currently did. The plants were full of brown leaves and drooping green ones. Cassie mentioned her busy schedule. She drew attention to the three plants and recollected how they were looking about as attractive as they had the day her mother-in-law decided to come for an unexpected visit. Cassie continued with her story.

Nancy had not been over for three weeks. She usually called Cassie the day before she planned on visiting. This particular time, Nancy called a couple of hours before. Cassie had hung up the phone and, after studying her three sick plants, made her decision. Cassie was not in the mood for an instruction, so she marched to the garden shop a short distance away and bought three plants, the same kind as her dying ones. Cassie hurried home, hung up the plants, cleaned up the house, and waited for her mother-in-law to arrive.

When Nancy walked into the front room and spotted the

Lao Tzu Tao said, "A great nation is like a great man: When he makes a mistake, he realizes it. Having realized it, he admits it. Having admitted it, he corrects it. He considers those who point out his faults as his most benevolent teachers. He thinks of his enemy as the shadow that he himself casts."

When good bonds are created with each other, there is more support, love, and time. Children also have more support and love. Less fighting between spouses over parental issues permits more support. Children gain a support system with stronger bonds of love that cannot be destroyed.

When there is greater understanding, people develop more tolerance, patience, flexibility, and respectfulness. Life moves forward, and we find our role has changed. Suddenly we are faced with becoming the mother-in-law. It can be handled and survived. The course has already been walked but on the other side of the road. Making some mistakes will only increase our understanding if we think the errors through and. remember what George Bernard Shaw said, "A life spent making mistakes is not only more honorable but more useful than a life spent doing nothing."

Story 7

"Doing an injury puts you below your enemy; revenging one makes you but even with him; forgiving sits you above him." - *Prochnow*

Cassie was an easy woman to talk with. She began her rendition on her mother-in-law Nancy. Cassie had been married to Sean for over ten years. Cassie had a twinkle in her eyes every time Nancy's name was mentioned. She gestured towards her lush plants and recalled one particular account about her plants and her mother-in-law. Cassie began her story with an amused smile.

When Cassie and Sean had been married for about five

meal is thrown together from a box. Other mothers-in-law stated that if they just dropped by unexpectedly, they got a cold shoulder. They did not feel welcome. Some mothers-in-law felt like intruders in their son's home.

The truth for both mothers-in-law and daughters-in-law lies someplace in the middle. There are imperfections in the best of us but also worthiness in the worst of us. If we display appreciation, we might be more considerate in our opinions. Achieving an appreciation for another's challenges allows us to appreciate and be conscious of them.

Many mothers-in-law agreed boxed pizza was just fine as long as they got an invitation to come over, the company was the important part. Both factions wished for pleasant conversation.

When both women support and share their own argument and it does not change each other's mood, they must admit to a compromise. They have opinions, but they have to get over the bump and move forward. They can accept their differences and keep the friendship strong. Nobody sees all things in the same way. Strength and confidence in making decisions takes courage. Children are taught to include others and to share and take turns when they play, yet adults don't practice what they teach.

Mothers-in-law are used to being their son's advisor. They have raised and nursed him through illnesses and emotional states. His happiness is vital to them. The playing field changes when the son has a girlfriend and things evolve quicker when she becomes his wife. The mother-in-law must learn the rules of the new game.

Mothers of girls are exempt from the necessity of needing to learn a new game. Jealousy can be a concern when a mother-in-law or daughter-in-law fuels the flames. Daughters-in-law who are patient have a better chance of maintaining a harmonious relationship with the mother-in-law. Likewise, a mother-in-law should not assume her daughter-in-law is too young to be correct in her assessment.

Chapter 6 – Respect Mistakes

"Be kind, for everyone you meet is fighting a hard battle." - *Plato*

"A moment of anger can destroy a lifetime of work! Whereas a moment of love can break barriers that took a lifetime to build." - *Anonymous*

A daughter-in-law's fairness to her mother-in-law is partly out of respect for her husband. Becoming aware of others plants the seeds for nurturing and respect. Mothers-in-law and daughters-in-law are hurt by words and actions.

Being mindful of another's state of mind permits us to empathize with what they might be pondering or feeling. A mother-in-law might be unaware when her daughter-in-law has been up all night with a crying baby. A daughter-in-law might share this information.

A daughter-in-law might focus into her mother-in-law's complaints. Her mother-in-law may not always feel well, and a daughter-in-law might consider all of this before judging her mother-in-law's frame of mind.

Sometimes through common sense we demonstrate respect. Helping a mother-in-law clear off a table is appreciative. The little things mothers-in-law and daughters-in-law do for each other create the bonds of respect they have for each other.

We can reject our mother-in-law's concepts about house and childcare without rejecting her. We can never be too sure our way is the better way for doing things just because it is the current thinking.

Some mothers-in-law complain they never get invited to their daughter-in-law's house for dinner. If they do get invited, the

Questions for the Daughter-in-Law

- Do you compare the gifts you receive from your mother-in-law to the ones she gives to her daughter?

- Do you question your mother-in-law about family matters?

- Do you make your husband crazy with questions or innuendos about his mother?

- Do you believe your husband should never confide in his mother?

- Do you feel your husband gives too much time and attention to his mother?

- Can you speak your mind with your mother-in-law and meet in the middle?

Reflections for Daughters-in-Law

- Your husband loves his mother. His roots began with her, and she is a part of his history.

- Refrain from wounding and demeaning your mother-in-law. A well-intentioned compliment will go a lot further.

- Your mother-in-law is part of a different generation. Respect her difficulty accepting the new attitudes.

- Competing with your mother-in-law creates a no win situation. Keep everyone's sense of worth intact.

- Keep your own sense of worth alive.

- Nurture the love and closeness you have with your husband.

- Appreciate your husband's attention.

Helen saw no signs of Jim taking another job and, since Norma's promotion, there were no signs of Norma quitting hers. Helen became the permanent babysitter.

Discussion 6

"Money cannot buy peace of mind. It cannot heal ruptured relationships, or build meaning into a life that has none." - Richard M. De Vos

It is important to have all the facts when agreeing to any long-term arrangements. This story proves that point. There was no time limit to these sitting arrangements. Helen was given no tangible end to the job, and she was rendered to sense guilt if she didn't help Jim and Norma. Lisa and John were jealous of the arrangement Norma and Jim had. After all, they reasoned, Norma and Jim were paying little for excellent child-care. Helen had to provide the same child-care for John and Lisa. She couldn't show favorites towards her grandchildren.

Neither daughter-in-law considered the welfare of their mother-in-law. They paid no attention to the strain it was causing. Because Helen wanted to keep peace and not show preferences, she was caught in the middle of a jealousy struggle. Helen was not responsible for their money problems. As sad for them as Helen felt, she should not have taken on the responsibility without a reprieve. Both daughters-in-law were competing for their mother-in-law's time, attention, and services. Both couples played on Helen's guilt.

"More than jealousy or possessiveness pettiness kills love." - Marty Rubin

Story 6

"Submission is not about authority and it is not obedience; it is all about relationships of love and respect." - Wm. Paul Young

Helen was exhausted from taking care of her three grand-children. Her eldest son Jim was trying to get a carpentry business going. There wasn't a lot of money, so Jim depended on the extra money his wife's paycheck brought in. To save money, Jim asked his mother, Helen, to baby-sit temporally. The children were young, but Jim and his wife Norma had no choice. Jim believed it was going to be temporary. It was important for Norma keep her job because they were also depending on her medical insurance. The baby was plagued with a chronic ear infection, a constant reminder of their need for medical insurance. The fundamental truth was, they both needed to be working.

The children were one, three, and four. The baby-sitting was difficult for Helen, but Jim had promised as soon as a good job came along he would take it. Helen never questioned what Jim's idea of a good job was. Jim said when he got a good job Norma would quit her job and stay home with the children until they were of school age. That was the original plan. Three years later, Helen was still baby-sitting. Norma received a promotion and loved her job.

Helen was coping when her second son John, approached her with a request. John asked Helen if she would baby-sit for his six-month-old daughter. His wife Lisa stood at his side and waited for Helen's reply. Helen hesitated. Lisa retorted how Helen was in such a routine with Norma's children that one more shouldn't make a difference. Helen had no choice but to reply affirmatively. If she had baby-sat for Jim for three years already, how could she say no to John? After replying, she heard her two daughters-in-law giving each other a high five in the corner of the room. Both of them were laughing and whispering.

Narrow Minded Gossip

"In marriage, with children, at work, in any association-an ounce of praise of sincere appreciation of some act or attribute can very often do more than a ton of fault finding. If we look for it, we can usually find in even the most unlikely, unlikable and incapable person, something to

commend and encourage." – Anonymous

Perhaps one should question why they feel the need to trash others. Again the use of the word trash makes us uncomfortable. Gossip is a release of unnecessary rumor and a waste of time. We may be stressed out with our mothers-in-law and, if it gets to be overwhelming, the need to release anger is strong. This leads us to gossip. Whatever the reasons are, it causes us to focus on fault-finding which becomes the fuel that lights the fire.

Dispersing words and actions begins the hassle. On a bad day, anger builds up the intensity of the words and actions. The in-laws may be innocent of the accusations, but they can't defend themselves when they are not present during our gossiping moments.

"These are the few ways we can practice humility: To speak as little as possible of one's self. To mind one's own business. Not to want to manage other people's affairs. To avoid curiosity. To accept contradictions and correction cheerfully. To pass over the mistakes of others. To accept insults and injuries. To accept being slighted, forgotten and disliked. To be kind and gentle even under provocation. Never to stand on one's dignity. To choose always the hardest." - Mother Teresa

The Daughter-in-law's Mother

"Envy is a littleness of soul, which cannot see beyond a certain point, and if it does not occupy the whole space, feels itself excluded." - Wm. Hazlitt, characteristics 1823

The mother of the daughter-in-law should not be left out of the combination of those people who can inject confusion and stress into the relationship. She might hold the recipe for success or failure in the relationship her daughter has with her mother-in-law. Mothers may influence their daughters against becoming too close with their mothers-in-law because of their own insecurities. They may feel threatened by any positive relationship their daughter has with her mother-in-law. They might influence and insist that their daughter keep her mother-in-law detached from any genuine emotional closeness. A lot of love and support is lost when this occurs.

Mixed feelings consume the daughter-in-law, but if she can work through this, there is a possibility of a strong alliance between herself and her mother-in-law. Some daughters-in-law believe it is impossible to crawl out from their mother's grasp and take charge of their own lives. All parents have the power and ability to instill guilt in their adult children. The mother-in-law daughter-in-law relationship is not exempt.

The potential for a happy and positive relationship is lost when there is no room for all kinds of love and affection. Elizabeth O'Connor stated, "Envy is a symptom of lack of appreciation of our own uniqueness and self-worth. Each of us has something to give that no one else has." The words beg us to appreciate our individuality as well as the individuality of others.

It is important to realize your husband is a part of your mother-in-law. There is room in his heart to love many people. Nobody can expect they should fill up the entire area. Perhaps you are creating a problem in the relationship right from the beginning when you display feelings of anger. A daughter-in-law must have confidence in herself and her place in the scheme of things.

It is not up to the daughter-in-law to try to fathom her mother-in-law's jealousy, but to recognize and accept it. By applying more effort into witnessing her mother-in-law's virtues, she sets a positive bond in motion. A daughter-in-law may grant her mother-in-law the benefit of the doubt about past decisions which were made at a different period in time. Likely they were made with conviction, given the circumstances. One cannot imagine or understand that phase in the mother-in-law's life. It is easy to use hindsight and publicly state she made poor decisions. Comprehending and accepting the mother-in-law's decisions, allows one to be liberated from their own present and past choices. As Plutarch said, "To find a fault is easy; to do better may be difficult."

Ambitions are personal and need to be revised regularly. Setting goals and reaching them takes courage. Objectives can be accomplished. Motivation forces us to strive and live up to our goals. Major decisions that hurt and belittle another person make us aware of the consequences of our actions. Some people hide the labor better than others and some complain less, but the grind is enduring for all of us and accountability lies with everyone.

tions of situations.

New mothers-in-law are at their most vulnerable period in the beginning. They are perhaps unaware of the impact their bonds with their sons have on their new daughters-in-law. Perhaps the daughter-in-law's acknowledgment of the tremendous effect the mother-in-law has on her husband is a crucial affirmation of acceptance. Daughters-in-law might find life more tranquil if they treaded lightly and bestowed smaller amounts of criticism, if any at all, with regard to their mothers-in-law.

Most people love their mothers regardless of their mothers' faults. If we would not criticize our friends' mother, we may reconsider whether or not scattering negative comments about our mother-in-law is a good thing to do. At this point we must ask ourselves why do it? Do we feel inferior or fragile in the presence of our mother-in-law? Does she intimidate us? These are important questions to be mulled over. It is hard to forgive someone we don't understand.

Mothers nurture their children through the ordeals of physical and emotional illness. Constant reproaches or disapprovals of anyone's mother would drive a wedge into a friendship of any kind. The love a husband and wife have for each other is stronger, but it will not withstand a barrage of insults lodged against ones' mother. The marriage may be stressed beyond repair.

The man might overlook the deriding remarks and refrain from challenging his wife, but he will question why his wife would hurt him so profoundly. The daughter-in-law who cannot control her remarks may find she has created a situation extremely painful for all concerned.

The same daughter-in-law who might not like the help her mother-in-law gives to her husband will readily accept help for herself from her own mother. There is a different set of rules. The husband is the unwilling pawn and the mother-in-law the unwilling player.

Son Praises Mother

"Don't waste your time with explanations: people only hear what they want to hear." - Paulo Coelho

When we are jealous, we are not being ourselves. Most often we sabotage our individual merit. Our husbands and sons cannot behave in their normal way because they know they are being closely monitored. Husbands are possibly resented by their wives, if they praise their mothers and possibly begrudged by their mothers if they praise their wives. Harmony is non-existent in these situations, but we can alter the situation because, as George Elliot professed, "It is never too late to be what we might have been."

Getting beyond the jealousy and recognizing each woman's significance, is worth the time and effort. Discussions, observations, and stories show most sons have developed a playful attitude with their mothers as a carryover from childhood. When one watches the interaction, it is easy to observe the loving light-heartedness between a mother and her adult son. Exploring this through a daughter-in-law's eyes, one might see a rival that possibly should be crushed.

The mother-in-law is, understandably, the "other" woman. A son that might compliment his mother's cooking may be encountered with scornful glaring eyes. One might ask what the son learns from these interactions. He remembers to stop complimenting his mother in front of his wife if he wants peace with his wife. There are some daughters-in-law who might save the argument surrounding the praise for the car ride home. In these cases, the treatment of the situation may appear to be lighthearted, but it may still remain caustic as the dinner and the mother-in-law are reviewed and discussed during the car ride home. Whenever you are in conflict with someone, there is one factor that can make the difference between damaging your relationship and deepening it, and that factor is attitude. Our attitude testifies to the importance of our own percep-

Chapter 5 – Jealousy is Poisonous

"Real love is the moment you believe that love is not about losing or winning. It is just a few moments in time, followed by an eternity of situations to grow from." - *Shannon Alder*

Jealousy manifests in numerous areas and in an endless range of circumstances. A daughter-in-law can be jealous of the attention her mother-in-law gives to her son, another daughter-in-law, or the mother-in-law's daughter. A daughter-in-law may dislike her husband's attention to his mother.

The daughter-in-law's mother might resent any close relationship her daughter has with her mother-in-law. The list of the circumstances in which jealousy might be visible is infinite. Jealousy may often arise when there are grandchildren. A mother-in-law perhaps feels she does not have the same kind of access to the children that her daughter-in-law's mother has.

Some mothers-in-law complained their daughter-in-law put words in their mouths and interpreted everything they said to their husbands. The way it came back to the mother-in-law was not always what she said or meant to get across. The mothers-in-law were frustrated because they saw this as a deliberate attempt to make them appear to be in the wrong and to be a bad person in their sons' eyes. Even small remarks were twisted into something beyond what was actually implied. Toba Beta said, "Jealousy is love in competition," which to me depletes the love rather than increases it.

Questions for the Daughter-in-Law

- Are your mother-in-law's gifts perceived as thoughtless?
- Do you like your mother-in-law's gifts more when you know the cost?
- Do you believe your mother-in-law should share some of her wealth so you and your husband could get a start on life?
- Have you ever questioned your mother-in-law's appreciation of your gifts?
- Do you recognize time given as a gift?
- Have you considered asking for things you want to alleviate unwanted gifts?

Reflections for Daughters-in-Law

- There is an emotional cost if you borrow money from your mother-in-law. Repay when you can.
- Save whatever amount of money you can each month for desired or unexpected items.
- Live within your means. Material items can wait. You will be a happier person.
- Appreciate money your mother-in-law gives to you.
- Respect your mother-in-law 's right to do what she wants with her money.
- Do not compare your mother's gifts to your mother-in-law's gifts. You cannot put prices on love.
- Consider time your mother-in-law gives to you worth more than money.
- Stay out of the discussion when there is a money problem between your husband and his mother.

It is easy to make assumptions. It is critical for families to discuss problem situations that manifest. Many needless arguments are actually unfounded. Peace can easily be found again with open honesty.

"When the one great scorer comes to write against your name-he marks- not that you won or lost but how you played the game." - Grantland Rice

Money Misery

It is not always wise to borrow money from one's parents. If a couple chooses to borrow money, a payment schedule should be set up immediately. All parties should agree to the conditions, and there should be no unstated requisites. Brian had assumed whenever his mother had a request he had to jump and do it right away. Brian put this pressure on himself. He forgot his mother chose to lend him the money. She did not put any demands to the agreement. Brian suffered with anxiety, and the guilty conscience made him respond promptly. He distressed himself.

Amy made her own assumptions because Brian had become uncommunicative. She concluded Ann was hassling Brian to do the many jobs. Amy blamed Ann and began resenting her. Ann and Amy had a good relationship before the borrowed money. Amy should have voiced her complaints to Ann instead of fueling the smoldering anger. She finally lashed out at Ann and caused everything to erupt, which was actually a good thing.

Ann tried to help Amy and Brian. Ann should have paid better attention to Brian's response time. She might have discovered his guilt and the overstretched tenseness it placed on his shoulders. Ann was so happy to have things done swiftly she did not consider Amy, who was waiting patiently at home. Ann should have been more aware of Brian and Amy's increasing resentment. Their anxious emotions were at the surface and simple to recognize. However, Ann might have been attempting to overlook the couple's edginess.

Amy and Brian could have mentioned their concerns sooner, but this family is to be commended for confronting their problems and manifesting a positive outcome. Brian and Amy took control of their lives again and set up a payment schedule. They aimed to pay back the money they owed to Ann as soon as they could. They did not want Ann to think they were doing things for her out of the guilt of owing her. Amy and Brian loved Ann and sought to assist her when they could. Both households began functioning smoothly again.

confused. Ann couldn't figure out why they hadn't just told her that they had plans. Ann cowered into her armchair. Amy relented when she saw her mother-in-law's frail frame quiver. Amy sighed as the tears rolled down her cheeks also.

Ann apologized in a broken voice, for the couple's ruined plans. Brian entered the room and tightened his face as he looked at the two women. Brian broke the silence. "I owe you mom," He said. Ann was shocked, and saddened. She had not meant for her gift to place such restrictions on Amy and Brian. All three had a lot of issues to discuss. There was relief all around.

"We make a living by what we get. But we make a life by what we give." - Sir Winston Churchill

Discussion 5

"I have learned from experience that the greater part of our happiness or misery depends on our dispositions and not on our circumstances." Martha Washington

Ann, Amy, and Brian reflected on the situation. They sat down together and communicated their various considerations. Ann admitted being surprised and shaken when she realized Amy and Brian felt guilty and indebted to her because of the borrowed money. Ann should have made it clear she was not expecting them to become obligated to her in any way. Ann explained she was telling Brian what had to be done as she had always done before. She was not in any way suggesting Brian do the jobs immediately. Ann had not meant to put a wedge in her relationship with her daughter-in-law and son. Amy felt relieved to discover Ann was not pressuring Brian to do more projects. Amy was sorry she had concluded, Ann's motives falsely.

47

Story 5

"What I gave I have; what I spent, I had; what I kept, I lost. "

- Old Epitaph

"Remember that time is money." - Ben Franklin

Brian and Amy were tired of paying the exorbitant rent. They couldn't seem to get ahead. Whenever they had a little bit of money saved up in their joint bank account, something in the house would need to be repaired. This realization forced them to take the money out of the bank and spend it. Amy wanted to buy a house. Brian wanted a house, but he was nervous about spending most of the saved money. He worried about unexpected emergencies. After discussions, they decided to ask Ann, Brian's mother, for a loan. Ann agreed immediately to give the couple money for a down payment on a house.

As the weeks passed, problems arose. Whenever Ann called for even the smallest problem as she had always done in the past, Brian would rush over to take care of it. Ann would mention it was not terribly important, but Brian would still arrive instantly. Ann was surprised at Brian's response time but she did not comprehend the reason behind it. Other incidents began to make Ann curious. She was surprised when Amy stopped dropping over for visits. Whenever Ann did see Amy, the conversations were curt and formal. Ann questioned Brian, but she never received any answers. Vincent Voilture said it best, "Fortune is a great deceiver. She sells very dear the things she seems to give us."

One day, Brian arrived at his mother's to fix a problem she was having with her car. Amy came with Brian and paced around the kitchen. Amy finally plunged into a chair, stomping her feet as she stretched. Ann questioned Amy's strange behavior and discovered she and Brian had been on their way to a movie. Ann was upset and

46

stand or worry that grandparent may be able to give more. This is a dilemma for the parents to solve. Sometimes an inexpensive thoughtful gift is cherished more than an expensive gift. Spending time with the children or babysitting them is an invaluable gift to offer.

Jane is behaving rudely to Ava, and this is another difficulty that Jill needs to deal with if she truly wants a solid and respectable relationship with her mother-in-law. The children will move towards an appreciation and love for their grandparents', provided they have opportunities to share precious moments together. Jane might attempt to play the games Ava gave to the kids, with her grandchildren. Kids will not equate their grandparents' love with the size or quantity of gifts. These concepts will be understood with time, and the children will be nobler for having acquired the lesson.

Jill is more troubled about her mother's reaction to Ava's gifts than she is bothered by the number of gifts given. If Ava's wealth is problematic for Jill, then she needs to rethink her own self-worth and feelings of inferiority Ava's wealth fosters. Ava should not be offended because of her wealth. Jill has to work on respecting Ava for who she is.

Ava seems to be innocent of seeking to deliberately annoy anyone with her offerings. She enjoys sharing her possessions with her grandchildren. It might be possible for them to reach a compromise. Jill might discuss some of her fears with Ava and resolve the issue. Everyone might work on a solution that promotes peace. As Ted Key said, "Every accomplishment large and small begins with the same decision: I'll try."

Jill is wavering between her mother and Matt's mother. Jill's mother has complained to Jill about the abundance of gifts from Ava, and Jill considers it necessary to justify her mother's viewpoints. People don't always have to fight as Shannon Alder explained, "The battle you are going through is not fueled by the words or actions of others; it is fueled by the mind that gives it importance."

Jill is grateful to Ava but can't show it because it would feel like a disloyalty to her own mother. Now Jill has been confronted by Matt's necessity of justifying his mother's feelings. Jill never considered Ava's feeling about anything. This is a new situation, and Jill is not sure how to handle it. Ava is caught in the middle of Jill and her mother, and Jill and Ava need space to communicate. It might be realistic for them to come to an understanding about the money and gifts. Ava could give her gifts to the children throughout the year. This could alleviate the huge pile of gifts given all at once. Ava could make some of her gifts monetary and place the money into an account for the kids for their future needs.

It's essential the children be taught the gift of time is a significant gift. Being excited to receive their grandmother's gifts may not teach them appreciation for gift giving. It is reasonable to assume when the children mature they will assign more emphasis on the human quality of the relationship rather than the monetary value. There may come a time when Ava is unable to purchase such gifts. Jill should be thankful for whatever she receives. A respectful and well-mannered person does not make anyone feel uneasy for any reason. Willa Cather emphasized one's nervous feelings when she said, "He had the uneasy feeling of a man who is not among his own kind and who has not seen enough of the world to feel that all people are in some sense his own kind."

If we are not equating money with love, Jill's mother should not feel degraded or threatened, because of what she cannot afford. It would be worthwhile for her to bear in mind she is buying gifts from her heart, and children do not know the cost of presents. When children are young, they love presents. They do not under-night Matt confronted Jill about the way she had treated his mother. Matt was tense, alert, and angry. Jill admitted she was always over-whelmed with Ava's abundance of gifts. Jill stated she appreciated Ava's gifts, but she never knew how to thank her in front of her own mother. Jill was also uncomfortable with the number of gifts Ava lavished on the children. Matt wasn't listening. He slammed the door and went for a walk. Jill glanced across the room and saw Lori and Mark busily playing with the new toys from Ava. Jill sat down on the edge of the bed and cried.

"Happiness is like a butterfly. The more you chase it, the more it will elude you. But if you turn your attention to other things, it comes and softly sits on your shoulder." - Nathaniel Hawthorne

Discussion 4

"Make a memory with your children, spend some time to show you care; toys and trinkets can't replace those precious moments that you share." - Elaine Hardt

Money is creating happiness and unhappiness. Ava spends money lavishly. She had little money growing up, so now it means nothing more to her than to spend it or give it away. Jill doesn't grasp the meaning Ava places on her money. Jill sees Ava's money as boastful. Jill is confused with Ava's spending because Ava is not seeking thanks or rewards for herself. Jill cannot grasp Ava's motives but does believes Ava has motives.

The confusion for Jill has more to do with the seeds of doubt her own mother Jane has planted. Jill is trying to protect her mother from the boastfulness of Ava's gifts. Jill doesn't dislike Ava and is not jealous of Ava. Jill is genuinely confused with all Ava gives.

Money Misery

Ava arrived at Matt and Jill's house loaded down with presents. Jill's mother Jane greeted Ava with a curt smile. Ava brushed past Jane and deposited her gifts on the kitchen table. Mark squealed when he saw Ava and all the presents. Ava immediately sat down at the kitchen table to enjoy a cup of coffee with Jane who was visiting from out of town. Jane had little to say to Ava and quickly maneuvered herself into another room away from Ave.

The children, Mark and Lori, opened the gifts from Ava and squirmed with delight. Jill encouraged them to open the gifts from their other grandmother. Whenever Mark opened a gift from Jane, there were explosions of delight from Jill. She praised the many beautiful books her mother had given to Mark. Jill told Mark and Lori she would read some of the new books that night before bedtime. Jill thanked her mother for the gifts but never thanked Ava. Ava was wounded.

Ava left Jill's house early and went home. She tried to make excuses for Jill and her mother Jane. Ava knew Jane was not wealthy, but maybe it was Jane's problem and not Ava's that it always ended up in a confrontation. Perhaps Jane was the one threatened by the gifts. Jane's the one equating gifts to affection, thought Ava. She has the issue, not me, she reasoned. Jill's mother could not afford expensive gifts. Jill's childhood was as frugal as Ava's childhood had been.

Still Ava was wounded by Jill's reaction to the presents. The only people Ava pleased was the children. She smiled because that was what it was all about anyway, and she didn't really care about assuming adults. Ava didn't have a semblance of hope at trying to comprehend Jill's attitude, but at the moment, she was low on sympathy. Ava had been insulted so many times it was difficult for her to feel any kindness towards Jill. All Ava could think about was how she'd grown up poor herself. You have to get over issues, she thought.

Ava confided some of her feelings to her son Matt. That

ing their marriage indebted to the mother-in-law or resentment can flourish. This might damage the relationship. Borrowing money creates land mines for all concerned. It is therefore advisable to borrow only in dire need and when all other options have been considered.

"A part of kindness consists in loving people greater than they deserve." - Joseph Joubert, French philosopher

Story 4

"A little thought and a little kindness are often worth more than a great deal of money." - John Ruskin

Ava was privileged to have enough money to splurge whenever she fancied. If her son Matt and his wife Jill needed any money, Ava was agreeable to give it to them. This appeared to be an ideal situation, but of course that was not the case. Ava indulged her grandchildren with gifts of toys and clothing on every birthday and holiday. Ava was pleased to be able to do this, but she was continually disappointed with Jill's reaction. Ava never flaunted her wealth and she never demanded anything in return. Ava didn't understand Jill's attitude. Ava wasn't forcing Matt and Jill to take any money from her. Ava only made it known she was there to help them if they required help.

Ava recalled her grandson Mark's birthday. Ava had bought Mark more presents than she could count. Ava always took such delight in the children's reaction to their gifts. Ava's father had died when she was young, so Ava had grown up poor. Pleasing her grandchildren was vitally important to her. It allowed Ava the pleasure of reliving her childhood through her grandchildren.

Chapter 4 – Money Misery

"Not he who has much is rich, but he who gives much."

- Erich Fromm

Money may contribute to arguments, unhappiness, and guilt. Money should never be equated with love. It may foster a desire in us for things we do not need. Money can contribute to selfishness, and although it is essential to life, it will never be an answer to problems.

People spend their childhood years growing up in homes where there are various amounts of wealth. Some people are more fortunate than others. Because of this and other variables, gifts given and the gifts received may differ. Many people are disappointed with the gifts from the in-law. It appears their present lacked thought. Some parents have more money and want to give their children as much as they can for as long as they can. This does not mean parents must give away their wealth.

If it becomes a necessity to borrow money from the mother-in-law, it is essential to be prepared and arrange for the emotional cost. Showing appreciation is important even if you will be reimbursing in the future. A mother-in-law cannot be expected to rescue the couple from every unpleasant situation even if she has the resources because there will be no growth.

If money is borrowed, a daughter-in-law may perceive any request from her mother-in-law as an obligation, even if that is not the mother-in-law's intention. A couple should refrain from start-

Questions for Daughters-in-Law

- Do you control your emotions when your mother-in-law invites you for a Holiday three months in advance?

- Do you accept your mother-in-law's gifts in good faith, even if you do not like them?

- Are you aware of and value your mother-in-law's traditions no matter how ridiculous they appear to you?

- Do you ever spend a Holiday with your husband's family?

- Do you ponder the gifts you buy for your mother-in-law with care?

- Do you make time throughout the year for visits with your mother-in-law?

Reflections for Daughters-in-Law

- Lend and appreciate help.

- Make an effort to visit your mother-in-law at other times during the year.

- Cherish your mother-in-law's traditions. They possess many memories.

- Be fair in dividing your time with respective families.

- Invite your husband's mother over.

- Gifts do not equate to value. Most of us choose a gift we want to receive.

- Search for quality and thoughtfulness.

- Accept your mother-in-law's traditions, even if they differ from yours.

- Believe love is shared and celebrated everyday not just on a Holiday.

ued, and scarcely given freely or often. When receiving the gift of time, people forget to say thank you, yet it is a gift you can't easily repay. As Irwin Federman stated, "People love others not for who they are, but for how they make us feel."

ask. Philip James Bailey explained it clearly when he said, "We live in deeds, not years, in thoughts, not breaths; In feelings, not in figures on a dial. We should count time by heart throbs. He most lives who thinks the most-feels the noblest-acts the best."

Gift Giving Nightmares

"The best rosebush after all is not that which has the fewest thorns but that which bears the finest roses." - Henry Van Dyke

Holiday gift giving can set off a nightmare. Gifts may propose affection but may not be useful. Most often the gifts we select for others is not what we receive. In most cases, gifts are certain to be disappointing. These gifts are not something we picked and should not be considered as evidence for how people feel about us.

Discussions suggest some daughters-in-law refuse to purchase anything for their mothers-in-law. They buy for their own mothers and often expect their husbands to do the same. This rationale is practical. A gift might constitute affection to the receiver and a reminder it came from the heart with love. Gift giving is not a competition in which the present is scrutinized as the largest, most expensive gift. A gift reflects caring and kindness.

One has to trust they were given in good faith. When a gift is purchased, the reflection ought to be about what the receiver prefers for herself and not what the buyer likes to get. Mothers-in-law and daughters-in-law should avoid judging the gift by the price tag. Gifts of time are the most valuable gifts. The small thoughtful things, which we say and do for each other throughout the year, are what matters most. If your mother-in-law is constantly helping you out with the dog and children, as well as inviting you for meals, she is no doubt worthy of your appreciation. The gift of oneself is the most generous gift we have to give. It is underestimated, underval-

Those who live at a distance must weigh traveling plans which increases the anxiety. Mothers-in-law may bring a pet when visiting, and this adds to the anxiety and confusion. With other adult children to consider, the mother-in-law may not want to travel at all. The problems and friction between the mother-in-law and daughter-in-law can easily intensify.

A new mother-in-law might put in more effort at securing her son and daughter-in-law's attendance for a holiday only to learn seeing them at some point during the holiday season is better than not seeing them at all. Discussions suggest most daughters-in-law maintain the second place position for their mothers-in-law. There is no other compromise that works. The mother-in-law may be happy to just be included in the festivities. Many daughters-in-law make an effort after the holiday. When daughters-in-law bring their pets, it often places burdens on the mother-in-law. She may want to see her son and grandchildren so badly she accepts the circumstances, which are an added burden.

Daughters-in-law may discount the amount of paraphernalia that accompanies them when they are visiting. Many dismiss the disruptions to the home. They do not perhaps consider the baby's items an intrusion. A living room may serve as a nursery, and a cherished coffee table may be used for food, bottles, and diapers. A mother-in-law's home becomes completely disturbed. Some mothers-in-law don't care while others complain and run the risk of being considered unloving and disinterested in their grandchildren.

Most mothers-in-law will put up with just about anything to spend time with their grandchildren. They will probably work around a baby's schedule or toddler's wants and needs, but it is important to respect your mother-in-law's home. By simply requesting where you might change the baby or feed the messy toddler, you are exhibiting respect which might be what your mother-in-law was seeking. Adoring her grandchildren doesn't mean a mother-in-law will appreciate a lack of respect the adults have displayed. The mother-in-law may offer no restrictions, but it is still important to

had a satisfying effect on all. Sometimes the solutions are simple, but occasionally there are no answers and whatever transpires must be dealt with. A daughter-in-law's own family might facilitate disagreements between couples.

In Lori and Kyle's situation, Lori championed a decision. This resulted in arbitration with her parents. The circumstances were not ideal, but the negotiating produced an equitable resolution.

Engaging everyone's participation to achieve a reasonable outcome for all, promotes satisfaction. Evidence suggests harmony precedes love. Being a bigger person requires compromise. Future insight allows one to grasp a positive outcome for a difficult dilemma.

When Mothers-In-Law Visit

" Riches and power are but gifts of blind fate, whereas goodness is the result of one's own merits." - Heloise

Mothers-in-law might choose to spend the holidays with their son and daughter-in-law. A daughter-in-law might be forced to accept the arrangements. Husbands need to become more involved when their mothers are visiting. It is important for them to contribute to their mother's comfort and to assist their wives with the arrangements and workload. It is beneficial for the wives to state their expectations and accept help from their spouse and guests.

Mothers-in-law, who live at a distance, require overnight accommodations. Close quarters may foreshadow unexpected problems, which evidence suggests, heightens the tension. It is good to remember what the Aesop Greek fabulist declared "No act of kindness, no matter how small, is ever wasted."

on the same day when they had to manage a two-hour drive. When Lori and Kyle were first married, they agonized over what to do every time there was a holiday. Lori was determined she and Kyle not fight about where to spend the Holidays so the traveling began.

One day Lori suggested to her mother, they celebrate the Holidays the week after the calendar Holiday. At first this sounded a little strange. Lori's siblings questioned the feasibility of working out the details in order to make it work. The siblings resolved to give it a try. The suggestion turned into a regular yearly happening. It was still effective after ten years. Lori's family was satisfied with the situation. It allowed them the freedom to visit with their in-laws, on the day of the Holiday without any hassles. Lori's family celebrated together after the Holiday in peace and quiet. It was one of the best things they had ever achieved. It is never about a calendar day, but the opportunity to share precious moments with those you love.

They had a wonderful time, and on no account were pressures applied. Anyone had the option to also attend the festivities at their mother's house on the day of the Holiday. Everyone's in-laws were quite gratified with the arrangement, which permitted them to plan their own celebrations. Lori and Kyle succeeded in eliminating Holiday demands

Discussion 3

"How far you go in life depends on your being tender with the young, compassionate with the aged, sympathetic with the striving and tolerant of the weak and the strong. Because someday in life you will have been all of these." -
George Washington Carver

Lori admired her mother-in-law and she welcomed being able to share two Holidays. Lori and Kyle considered their families and came out ahead. Lori empowered everyone. The compromise

attempt to visit with her at other times during the year might be appreciated.

If one judges the gifts they receive or anticipate quantity from the holidays or the gifts, they miss the spirit of the holiday. The person who donates their time and effort throughout the year deserves to be remembered. They are a true value. The thought of Toni Sorenson is powerful, "The spirit of Christmas is found when we lift the load of others."

Television and the media present us with images of happy sentimental scenes. They forget to add the loss of sleep, headaches, fussy baby, broken homes, loss of life, sickness, job loss, disagreements, sadness, confusion, distrust and lack of focus or direction. The Holidays constrain us even more when others cannot be pleased. When in-laws are a component to be considered, the anxiety is intensified.

Story 3

"I finally figured out that not every crisis can be managed. As much as we want to keep ourselves safe, we can't protect ourselves from everything."

Anonymous

Lori was thirty-years-old with short dark hair and a quick smile. Lori relished entertaining guests. It did not surprise Kyle, her husband, when she frequently invited the neighbors next-door. Kyle was accustomed to Lori's spur of the moment gestures. Lori came from a large family. She had four brothers and two sisters. Kyle had three siblings. At holiday time both of their respective families yearned to have them at the dinner table.

Lori and Kyle lived within two hours of both sets of parents, but it was frustrating and challenging to journey to two homes

Chapter 3 – Holiday Crisis

"Don't forget the small kindnesses and do not remember the small faults." -
Chinese proverb

The ability to hide fear is easier for some people, but without a doubt, nobody likes being criticized or gossiped about behind their back. None of us comprehend the total meaning behind words, actions, or gifts. Most people fret about their own situation, unaware of the heartaches they drop on others.

It is important to embrace each holiday. They have their own distinct moments; giving unconditionally, has never disappointed anyone. Equating the gifts from your mother-in-law to the value she places on your worth is a mistake. Most people choose a gift they would prefer for themselves and one they can afford.

Holiday traditions change and are a part of life. Changes occur when a child starts school, gets married, or goes to work or college. When people help each other with these transformations, they become less fearful. Even good changes are filled with stress. The traditions of your mother-in-law are worth respecting. They were developed over numerous years and possess many memories. She may be willing to let go of most of these traditions, but it is emotionally difficult.

Lending a helping hand when possible solves problems. Fairness in dividing time with the respective families makes for fewer complaints. Mothers-in-law deserve some attention. The mother-in-law has a difficult position, and she deserves some invitations at holiday gatherings. She is your husband's mother. If it is impossible to spend time with the mother-in-law during the holidays, an

31

Questions for Daughters-in-Law

- Do you ever agree to something in order to keep the peace?

- Have you doubted decisions you have made?

- Do you like proving your mother-in-law wrong? Why?

- Are your decisions influenced by the opinions of others?

- Would it bother you if your three-year-old child was not toilet trained?

Reflections for Daughters-in-Law

- Choose a plan of action, assert yourself, and follow through with your plans.

- It's okay to be wrong and to make mistakes, just learn from your mistakes.

- Reflecting on what others say is helpful, but one must have confidence in self.

- Never fear to state your opinions, even if they differ from your mother-in-law.

- A new way for doing things does not necessarily make it better.

- Your methods for raising children will be outdated in the future, so respect your mother-in-law's outdated ap proaches.

- Being independent is being able to admit someone else may be right.

- Being independent is not fearing being wrong.

- Don't get involved with your husband's disputes with his mother.

dren. Clearly, Emily has her own inhibitions to deal with here. The only recourse Emily has is to strongly state the conditions of her availability.

Manipulation can be powerful in controlling another. Pat subdued Emily and convinced her to baby-sit. Pat's agreement with Emily should have facilitated in Pat, a responsibility towards her mother-in-law. Emily required clear guidelines relating to restrictions and length of time for her services. Emily should have followed Pat's procedures for discipline and rules. Emily should have respected Pat's priorities rather than use the situation as an excuse to control her grandchildren.

When George's job was not in jeopardy, Emily's commitment to baby-sit should have ended. The conditions of the original agreement changed. The crises ended and required renegotiations. This should have allowed Emily to withdraw from baby-sitting but she couldn't articulate her needs.

George suffered through several months of distress. Emily was delighted to be of help. Stability eventually returned to George's company. His job was no longer in jeopardy. It was unnecessary for Pat to continue working, but she enjoyed her new job and refused to quit. Emily's knee deteriorated and her asthma worsened. The babysitting arrangements remained.

Emily questioned George every day about curtailing her babysitting. George astutely avoided her queries when he picked the children up after work. He habitually hustled the children out the door. Pat delivered the children to Emily in the morning. She eluded conversation and frowned at Emily's complaints while making excuses to rush.

Emily refused dinner invitations from Pat and George. Her bouts with asthma increased and her knee worsened, but she continued baby-sitting.

Discussion 2

"Courage is what it takes to stand up and speak; Courage is also what it takes to sit down and listen."

- Herbert V. Prochnow, and Herbert V. Prochnow Jr.

Our needs prioritize our choices. These choices should not suppress nor deprive others of their own necessities. Despite Emily's health problems, she accepted the job of caring for her grandchildren. It was difficult for Emily to ignore her son and daughter-in-law's request for help. Perhaps Emily did not consider that she was being manipulated, but she worried about being considered a mean mother-in-law if she refused to help. Emily also used the situation for her own advantage to discipline the children the way she saw fit. Emily didn't think about Pat's way of dealing with the chil-

Story 2

"It is not work that kills men but worry. Work is healthy; You can hardly put more on a man than he can bear. But worry is rust upon the blade. It is not movement that destroys the machinery but friction."

- Henry Ward Beecher

Pat and George had two children, a six-year-old named Jamie and a four-year-old named Todd. Pat was a stay at home mother, but she was recently feeling restless and anxious. Her husband's moaning about job layoffs at his company increased her edginess. George would come home from work, snatch the newspaper, and brood in front of the television set. His worrying affected his eating, and it heightened Pat's nervousness.

Pat resolved to get a job and contribute to the finances. Pat did not want her children in day-care, so she approached her Mother-in-law Emily. Likely Emily wanted to oblige, but she was afflicted with an arthritic knee and seasonal asthma. Pat did not consider these adversities relevant to Emily's decision. Pat trusted Emily's ability to care for the children and admired Emily's boundless energy. Emily never complained, so Pat saw no reason why Emily would refuse to baby-sit.

Pat disclosed her fears to her mother-in-law one day. Pat justified her return to the work force as anxiety over George's possible job loss. She affirmed this as the motivating factor. Subsequently, Emily agreed to baby-sit. Pat located a job in a short while and proceeded to work. Emily was a disciplinarian and believed Pat was too easy with the children. Emily made it her mission to get the kids to behave. Pat was not happy with this arrangement but felt helpless to speak her mind for fear of losing Emily as a babysitter. Emily took advantage of her situation and her empowerment and instilled her own rules and regulations with the children.

stressful days when a lending hand was welcomed.

Daughters-in-law want their husbands to notice them as efficient and capable individuals who have everything under control. At this point in their lives, mothers-in-law are more relaxed and confident about child rearing because they have already been there and done that. Daughters-in-law on the other hand are learning as they go but want to appear more confident on the outside while dismissing any angst they have on the inside.

Some daughters-in-law attempt to put their mothers-in-law in their place in order to get them to back off. They might even find fault with their husbands in the process. All the wonderful reasons which made this woman want to marry him in the first place are now overlooked. The mother-in-law is not given credit for her son's virtues but only his vices. Mothers-in-law might be blamed for many things, such as his habit of eating too quickly, his dislike of vegetables, his love for candy, and other faults. This criticism is possibly undeserved. It is a way of criticizing the mother-in-law's parenting skills.

Research shows that most mothers who attempt to perform all the right things still do not insure positive outcomes. Raising children and attending to one's marriage are daunting tasks not taken lightly by anyone. More than they know, mothers-in-law and daughters-in-law are on the same page. Most mothers-in-law could probably admit to countless and insurmountable issues they had to deal with when they were raising their children. The majority report it was the most difficult task to accomplish and never left them secure in the moment.

This should guide every mother away from expressing a criticism or complaint against another mother no matter what their generation. There will always be mistakes even if they differ from the previous generations. Henry Wadsworth Longfellow suggested we look inward for peace when he said, "Not in the clamor of the crowded street, not in the shouts and plaudits of the throng, but in ourselves are triumph and defeat."

25

One might question this logic, but it is irrelevant because independence is vital. The need to come to terms with our fear of change is imperative, like Lucan stated, "Thus each person by his fears, gives wings to rumor and without any real source of apprehension men fear what they themselves have imagined."

Some mothers-in-law are consigned to scheduled visits even though they have carefully avoided any transgressions. Wary daughters-in-law are not yet willing to take the chance of allowing their imperfections to be exposed.

Time and trust foster a friendlier relationship. When a daughter-in-law forbids her mother-in-law to ever stop by for a visit unless the visit is scheduled, she is encroaching on her mother-in-law's freedom to see her son. It is essential for both women to realize and accept this fact by cooperating with each other and allowing the relationship to move forward.

Husbands usually do not feel threatened by unannounced visits from their mothers-in-law; hence the daughter's mother is at times extended the courtesy of unscheduled visits. Husband's mothers are seen as judgmental, and more observant of household disarray. It is not important if this is truly the case or a subjective view of the daughters-in-law. What matters is how the daughters-in-law view visits from their mothers-in-law.

Some mothers-in-law have made the mistake of jumping in to help their daughters-in-law with a mundane task. They have been admonished. The mother-in-law feels she was only trying to assist, while the daughter-in-law sees this offer of assistance as an affront to her competence, especially if it is in front of her husband. Daughter-in-law may suffer an unreasonable amount of insecurity.

Many daughters-in-law attempt to portray an image of competence. They project the image of being able to handle anything, but they have not yet reached the stage of being able to let go and allow others to support them. Mothers-in-law are not thinking about incompetence. They simply desire to help. Most recall those

In these situations, our acceptance or refusal of help is up to us. There is no pressure either way. A sense of freedom to establish and play by our own rules is gained. Our ideas of independence, child care, money spending, and jobs succeed for us and that is what counts.

"Whatever your talent, use it in every way possible.... Spend it lavishly like a millionaire intent on going broke." - Brendan Francis

It is essential for some of us to have a garage, or a large kitchen, or an extra bedroom. Others prefer an apartment or condo. It happens that some women elect to stay at home with children and place their careers on hold while other mothers go straight back to work. There are those mothers who believe they have no choice regarding their decision.

Mothers who stay at home might be frowned upon. Most of us have the choice of child rearing at some point in our lives, and we must do what is right for us. A mother who is unhappy at home with the children ought to seek at least part-time employment. That is far better than feeling out of control and impatient with the kids. Some husbands leave the brunt of the childcare to the woman whether she is working or at home. This renders her exhausted at the end of a week. Independence is having the freedom to select what's best for us and to have those choices respected.

Mothers-in-law have had complete access to their children through all the years of child rearing. They continue to have this freedom of access even beyond college and into their adult child's first apartment. What most parents are not considering is the juncture where the adult child has a significant other person in their life. At this stage, if not sooner, the adult children need and want the freedom to live their own lives.

Privacy, rules, and scheduling become a necessity. It is possible a daughter-in-law's mother does not have the same restrictions.

Chapter 2 – Triumph and Defeat

"Isn't it kind of silly to think that tearing someone else down builds you up?"- Sean Covey

The word strong-minded creates images of a determined, self-sufficient, unconventional, and self-reliant person. Traits that are well developed and traits that need to be developed are found in all of us. Having our own way of doing and saying things makes us unique individuals. In many ways, it makes us irreplaceable. However, if we want to gain more knowledge, it is wise to listen now and again as is said in Proverbs, "Listen to advice and accept instruction, and in the end you will be wise."

It is not necessary to live in each other's homes, only to visit each other's homes. If a mother-in-law chooses to have her home flawless, then that is her choice. Respecting our choices is respecting our individuality. Some dogs are allowed to sleep on couches while other dogs are confined to kitchens.

Generally, all mothers-in-law and daughters-in-law want to make good impressions on each other. Neither is anxious to irritate the other or to cause problems. When a daughter-in-law tries too hard to make a good impression, she runs the risk of saying too much or possibly appearing insincere. Some daughters-in-law are nervous and say too little, which makes them appear distant. Henry James explained it simply, "All intimacies are based on differences."

Visits with our mothers-is-law make us modify ourselves in a variety of ways. Role-playing according to the circumstances and people we happen to be with is a common occurrence. The words and tone adopted at work is different from the more relaxed speech used at home. By being relaxed and without plans for a confrontation, we deplete the anxiety and uphold serenity.

Questions for Daughters-in-Law

- When your husband visits his mother, do you expect him home at a certain time?

- Do you rebel if your husband begins chores for his mother before he completes the jobs at home?

- When your husband is planning a visit to his mother who lives at a distance, do you altar the plans in any way?

- Do you mention the expense of a baby-sitter before asking your mother-in-law to baby sit?

- Do you ever veto plans your husband makes with his mother?

- Do you like to know well in advance when your mother-in-law is coming to visit?

- Are you flexible with last minute changes of plans your mother-in-law makes?

Reflections for Daughters-in-Law

- Allow your husband time to interact with his mother and family of origin.

- Your husband's family structure is already established, so accommodate it gradually and refrain from judgements.

- Extend hospitality towards your mother-in-law even with an unexpected visit.

- Discuss issues openly with your mother-in-law. Welcome different opinions with respect.

- Appreciate and respect your mother-in-law's busy life when she is unavailable.

- Your husband can love you and his mother at the same time.

- Holiday's promote family love and enjoyment. Arrange ments made in advance alleviate some issues.

- Don't look for faults. Criticism is never a good choice.

Discussion 1

"Make the best of what is in your power, and take the rest as it happens."
- Epictetus

Power and control dominate this conflict. Abby's parents rebelled against changes. They were content to eliminate alternatives. Declining Adam's offer, they anticipated the couple's compliance.

Abby's parents should have been more cognizant of Adam's wishes. More thought could have fostered a harmonious settlement. Abby might have expressed her distress to her parents long before it resulted in Adam's despair. She tried to command the situation using the old complaints. The arguments did not achieve the usual results.

Although Adam's parents had many members to share their celebration, they lamented Abby and Adam's absence. When Abby's attempts to convince Adam failed, she surrendered and deferred to Adam's wishes. Adam obviously was harboring emotions of discontent for quite some time. Prior to reaching his limit of anger and exploding, an arrangement to discuss his sentiments might have been achieved with less disturbance and upset. Peaceful communication should not be undervalued. It is reasonable to acknowledge the influence of group sanctioning. A couple can achieve arbitration by respecting each other's desires.

iday with his family. Abby was upset, confused, and in the middle. It wasn't that she disliked Adam's family or didn't want to spend the Holiday with them. She could not see any other way to solve this problem. Abby had silently prepared her speech to Adam and tossed the words from her lips in quick succession.

The old argument that Adam's family had so many members that the two of them would hardly be missed caused Adam to explode. He assured her he was not just one of a crowd but an individual who counted with his family. He contended they were each missed by his family at the Holidays. Adam professed his disappointment. He explained his annoyance at what he perceived as Henry and Alice's ability to pressure their daughter.

Abby's ploy at dispensing guilt on him fired Adam's resolution. He was determined to spend this Holiday with his family regardless of what Abby wanted. She could spend it with her own family, but his intensions were now fixed. He was going to participate in the Holiday festivities with his own family this year.

Adam stated the advancing ages of his own parents. Abby was unhappy, but she finally realized how important it was to Adam. She reasoned she had few choices, given Adam's state of mind. She acquiesced to go to Adam's family for the Holidays. She knew her parents could also attend, so the blame was really on them if they chose to spend it alone.

The invitation was extended three weeks in advance to Alice and Henry. Abby and Adam were surprised when Abby's parents declined the invitation. When Adam and Abby confronted Alice, she mustered excuses complaining about the car ride and her failing health. Abby questioned her mother about her health. Alice admitted she'd been having some chest pain and some difficulty breathing. Alice confided to Abby and Adam the doctor had scheduled her for various tests after the Holidays.

Abby sunk into the closest chair, blankly staring out of the window and biting her lips. Adam, who had been standing, stiffened his stance and refused to sit down at Henry's request. Adam glared at Alice and Henry as he stoically suffered defeat once again.

Henry interrupted the silence, "I think I should give you kids your Holiday check early so you can go shopping," he said. Henry proceeded to write a check. With faltering steps, Henry gave Abby the check. Adam gritted his teeth and squeezed the chair top he was leaning on. He tried to maintain composure but found it impossible. As an Australian nurse once said, "He who angers you conquers you." Adam's heart began to race. The check was a ritual every Thanksgiving. Henry insisted Abby get the money early so she could use it for Holiday shopping. Adam wished they would just wait for the Holiday like everyone else.

Adam yanked his coat off of the rack, tossed it over his shoulder, and without a thank you, shoved the door open and abruptly departed. With long quick strides, he reached his car door, yanked it opened, and gently sank into his seat. He yanked it again, harder, and the door slammed shut. Abby expediently said her good byes and raced in pursuit after Adam. Abby was as upset as Adam and was rethinking her decisions. Edward Tryon once said, "He that never changes his opinions never corrects his mistakes and will never be wiser on the morrow than he is today."

Adam was furious and distressed. He and Abby fought all the way home. He refused to alter their decision to spend the Hol-

have taken away our thinking and our senses. We are behaving like a robot who acts according to the buttons pushed. None of us want that for our adult kids. Parents must give the adult kids space as well as independence.

Story 1

"One should always play fairly when one has the winning cards."
- Oscar Wilde

Abby was an only child. When she first met Adam, she was thrilled with his home-life, which was a constant flurry of commotion. Adam was one of five siblings and Abby fell in love with Adam's whole family. They loved her in return, but the Holidays inevitably caused the need to make emotional decisions. Adam believed there was never any decision because they always spent the Holidays with Abby's parents. Abby felt bound to spend the Holidays with her family. Being an only child, she never even questioned the plan. Abby never realized the impact it was having on Adam.

When the Holidays approached, Adam got sullen and uncooperative. He never outwardly complained because he knew Abby's parents, Alice and Henry, would be alone if they did not share the Holidays with them, his heart was heavy when he thought about his own family and the festivities. Despite his agreement to spend it with Alice and Henry, he was becoming more resentful. Adam felt ignored because he had no voice in the decision and his heart filled with anger.

Frustrated with his lack of input, Adam felt helpless. One year; Adam requested they spend Thanksgiving with his family, and suggested they include Abby's parents. Adam had already asked his mom, and he knew Abby's parents would be more than welcome.

might allow for lenience towards her mother-in-law's input even if it is never followed.

It would be silly to refrain from listening to solid information out of jealousy or insecurity. It would be just as ridiculous to follow unworthy advice out of allegiance. Sometimes a daughter-in-law tends to ask and follow her parent's advice yet challenges the advice of her husband's parents. This is a dilemma. The couple must trust each other. Every couple has their own needs for a healthy union. The marriage grows stronger and the couple gains confidence by solving their own problems. Outside influences including one's parents, can be harmful to a marriage.

Bickering about whose parents to visit and or share an evening with is full of anxiety. Have fun and stop keeping a tally. Tallies place us at the mercy of others telling us what to do. I am not suggesting we frown upon one family over the other, but list making will fail on many levels.

Some people visit families and spend days with them. It is a twenty-four seven visit. There are some couples who have large family gatherings and of course have little one on one time with anyone. Others have small families and have lots of one on one time. I would not worry about offending but live in the moment. Being aware and appreciating what we have brings more serenity and love into our lives without any doubt.

Trying to satisfy our first family as if we had to maintain an allegiance poisons other relationships. We question every move and find it necessary to endow our own parents with being the first at everything. This I know gets tiring and stressful, and we don't need that stress.

Love has nothing to do with first or last or three days or three hours. We haven't betrayed our own families of origin because we love or care for our in-laws. Truthfully, when you attempt to cage love, it sours and dies. Love must be free and allowed to spread its wings. Whenever we peg ourselves into this hole of deception, we

isn't easy to stop abruptly. She may be trying but mostly slips back into her routine and faces glaring anger. More than anything, she wants this young woman to like her, but she just can't seem to do or say the right things. She fears losing her son and believes he is already slipping away. The harder she tries, the more she devastates the friendship with her daughter-in-law. She can sense her daughter-in-law's jealousy as well as her own. Bertrand Russell said it best: "The degree of one's emotion varies inversely with one's knowledge of the facts. The less you know, the hotter you get."

Decisions

"People only see what they are prepared to see."
-Ralph Waldo Emerson

Decision-making in a marriage ideally includes collaboration. An equal marriage weaves honesty and respect. Most couples upon marriage set up their own family unit. This allows for a separation from both sets of parents. Separate living quarters provides detached transactions.

A couple needs to trust each other and work together to make their situation successful. A solution to a problem is possible when a couple relies on each other's ability to resolve it. An achievable goal is the confidence that must enter into the couple's marriage. Accepting advice and then deciding if it is pertinent is worthwhile. Whether a couple decides to use that advice is their choice.

Love as a tool may be used as a manipulator for power. A young man who is anxious to please his wife will be only too happy to say and do whatever it is she wants. Most often if a young woman is aware of her own parent's influence in her decision making, it

Power Struggle

"Love is as necessary to human beings as food and shelter; but, without intelligence, love is impotent and freedom unattainable." - Aldous Leonard Huxley

Wives have the ability to bias their husband's beliefs. The man, who is caught in the middle of this power struggle, remains the intermediary between his wife and his mother. Neither woman should intentionally manipulate the man. A person cannot function forever out of anxiety or self-reproach. Many times mothers and wives are not aware of or thinking about the man they both love. His emotional state about any given situation is not taken into account. He will suffer the wrath of whichever woman he scorns. This is a lot of stress on the young man.

It may also be possible that the mother is not trying to dump any guilt on her son. The son may simply want to please his mother, and in the process, he is torn between disappointing his wife and upsetting his mother. Mothers fear losing their sons and sometimes do and say ridiculous things to hide their insecurity. They want to insure their love for their son and his love for them remains intact.

Wives are totally oblivious to the many changes taking place in the mother-in-law's life. She is older and dealing with a possible age crises or an identity issue. She is without a mothering job and ousted from a position of trusted advisor. Now she is considered a manipulator and nuisance. It takes a toll because it is her "Baby" who is at the center of the problem.

The mother-in-law appreciates the fact that she must let go, but it has been so natural for her to step into her mothering role it

This gives a sense of power and respect to her mother-in-law, yet she has the final say.

With both women digging in their heels, it can become constant friction. Neither party will acknowledge the viewpoint of the other. Both choose to display their authority in the situation. This is extremely challenging for the husband who is caught between two women he cherishes. Disregarding the mother-in-law's point of view can become a grave mistake. She must be given time to adjust to the changing circumstances. Given some slack allows her the opportunity to understand and accept her misguided thoughts on the present events. She has been so used to being the one her son called upon for advice that it is difficult to turn it off.

If given some understanding, she may gradually rather than forcefully give up her interference. Both women have displayed respect for the other in the process and may become allies rather than enemies for life. It isn't as hard as it might appear. Power is not yelling or bullying others. It is acknowledgement of all.

The man who is at the center of the controversy is loved by both women. They should be willing to agree to disagree. Misunderstandings are the lead cause of the strife between the two women. Neither wants to have disagreements but both women have kept their feelings hidden for so long that they may explode without warning. Both women want to exert their power and control, and the moment the mother-in-law is already feeling more vulnerable and depleted.

Chapter 1 – Who's in Charge

"Don't smother each other no one can grow in the shade." - Leo Buscaglia

Children are taught by adults to include others and to share and take turns when they play, yet adults at times exclude others they don't deem as worthy. They don't measure up to our standards. Does the other person have the same kind of freedom to choose? Social intelligence should be attainable if we think and feel with the heart.

The daughter-in-law accepts her relationship with her husband as exclusive. They are capable and ready to make their own decisions, and the daughter-in-law does not want her mother-in-law's interference. She may refuse to make any compromises. By adhering to this rule, she prevents any kind of collaboration. She could win a friend if she willingly listened once in a while to the advice her mother-in-law offered and then made her own choice.

Prologue

The mother-in-law can maintain her son's love as well as enjoy her contact with future grandchildren. The mother-in-law treads on a new playing field, discovers the new rules, releases her anxiety and faces her fears with courage. She will find out secrets and answers to questions she yearns to ask. She learns how to become a trusted ally and friend to her daughter-in-law and enjoy a happier life experience.

The daughter-in-law can stop worrying about being controlled and dominated by her mother-in-law and release her worries of becoming the nasty whiner who is without influence. She overcomes her stress about the possibility of a nosy mother-in-law and her jealousy over the love her husband displays towards his mother. The daughter-in-law forges a new life of independence. She displays the new rules, releases her anxiety and faces her fears with courage. She is in a position to enjoy her confidence, authority, and independence.

Discover some hidden secrets and answers to the questions many daughters-in-law would like to ask. Read the book with reflection and become a trusted ally and enjoy a happier life experience. The alterations are slow but transform your life for the better.

Finally, listening to numerous women of all ages moan, as well as experiencing both roles of mother-in-law and daughter-in-law, allows me to identify clearly with the guilt and misconceptions of both the mothers-in-law and the daughters-in-law. There is a lot of emotional confusion in this relationship. Learn how to interpret the danger signs within the relationship before you have disharmony. Resolve the stresses and desires of both women when a wedding is imminent. Meet in the middle where there is plenty of love and make the in-law an ally rather than an enemy. The man in the middle has his roots and his wings.

need to share. That renewed reminder and my background research information led to harmonious relationships with my three daughters-in-law and my son-in-law. These relationships continually evolve as the years pass and grandchildren are added. There are guidelines offered within the book regarding the new changes when children enter the picture.

Strangely enough, I began my research as a daughter-in-law and finished it as a mother-in-law. I spent over twenty-five years interviewing and surveying numerous women. I discussed and answered questions about the in-law problems on TV shows and radio shows as well as magazine interviews. The issues remain similar across generations which is amusing as well as enlightening.

Both women may be expecting a difficult relationship because of the onslaught of negativity and gossip. Both mothers-in-law and daughters-in-law must release the stress and negative thinking of unverified beliefs.

This book reveals numerous true stories including reflections and questions of interest at the end of each chapter, that help foster a deeper perception in order to embrace a harmonious relationship. A support of ideas is offered to generate a more positive attitude in settling the issues that arise. The stories example alternate ways to avoid troubling situations. Power struggles and jealousies can be crushed. A happy relationship is possible and leads to a lifelong ally.

It is also possible for the mother-in-law to stop feeling like the meddling pest and learn how to cope with the changes. She can transform her life for the better, build up her confidence, and let go of the past as she embraces the unfamiliar road ahead. The transformation is slow and requires patience and time for her to release her command and let go of her jealousies. Space must be provided to her son and daughter-in-law as they embark on a new life.

embarked on a mission to make the relationship understandable so both the mother-in-law and the daughter-in-law would be more informed and live happier lives.

After I married, I saw firsthand how emotional it was to become a daughter-in-law. Having listened to so many grievances of mothers-in-law, I had some sense of what my mother-in-law must be feeling. Of course, until I became a mother-in-law, I never totally understood the depth of the transformation of my life.

During my teaching years at various schools, I continued my research of the issues between the in-laws. I also had some of my own gripes, so I began writing the first draft of the book. As the years passed, I developed a survey and found so many willing participants who offered to fill it out and agreed to verbally discuss the complaints with me. This gave me some serious insights into the conundrum. Everyone was willing to discuss it with me, but few wanted to have names publicly mentioned.

As more years passed my four grown children married. I have three daughters-in-law and one son-in-law. Now suddenly I was at the other end of the challenge. I recalled my notes on the complaints and problems in this significant relationship, but I still made some of my own mistakes and learned from them. I also understood how difficult the changes are for the mothers-in-law and how important it is that both women accept these changes. In a way, it is a death to the old way of life and a need to evolve with the new way.

I was reminded of my daughter-in-law years and how much I doubted myself and my position. I also recalled my yearning for complete independence. Although my mother-in-law was easy to get along with, I wished she could disappear in the earlier days of marriage. I assumed my mother-in-law could simply back off. Of course, she didn't, and now I understand why. The roles are intertwined and full of love on both sides. Perhaps that is why both women hang on tightly and with a sense of ownership.

I rediscovered what I learned in kindergarten about the

Prologue

"There are only two lasting bequests we can hope to give our children. One of these is roots; the other, wings." - W. Hodding Carter II

There is a huge but ignored problem in the mother-in-law daugh ter-in-law relationship, and it plays havoc within the family. The women do not identify with each other, yet they both love the man in the middle who is the husband or son. Both women appear to have trouble sharing his love. How easily they can unintentionally annoy or hurt each other without appearing to notice. That is one issue, and it has no simple or magical solution. The vision of the book is to convince the readers of the importance and benefits of a harmonious mother-in-law daughter-in-law relationship.

There are cruel jokes about crabby daughters-in-law or interfering mothers-in-law with bumper stickers that say "Caution mother-in-law in trunk." The mother-in-law's and daughter-in-law's insults are hurtful and only add tension to the unfounded fears of both women.

Caught in such a dilemma, many people are afraid to touch the subject. The truth is by looking at the fears one gets to analyze fact from fiction. What we imagine is not always reality.

I started my investigation unwittingly at sixteen when I began listening to the complaining mothers-in law and daughters-in-law whom I worked with daily. The more I listened to their grievances, the more interested I became in researching this subject. I began opening up the discussion with any women willing to discuss their criticisms. I never had to twist any arms and began getting more information than I requested. As the years went by, I continued my interviews and began writing down the information. I

7

Story 10	90
Discussion 10	91
Reflections for Daughters-in-Law	94
Questions for daughter-in-law	95
Chapter 10 - Children & Grandchildren	96
Appreciate Help	97
Methods	98
Story 11	99
Discussion 11	101
Reflections for Daughters-in-Law	104
Questions for Daughters-in-Law	105

Chapter 5 – Jealousy is Poisonous	52
Son Praises Mother	53
The Daughter-in-law's Mother	56
Narrow Minded Gossip	57
Story 6	58
Discussion 6	59
Reflections for Daughters-in-Law	60
Questions for the Daughter-in-Law	61
Chapter 6 – Respect Mistakes	62
Story 7	64
Discussion 7	66
Reflections for Daughters-in-Law	68
Questions for Daughters-in-Law	69
Chapter 7 – Overcome Fear	70
Self-Doubt	70
Fluidity of Status	71
Strength in Challenges	73
Story 8	74
Discussion 8	76
Reflections for Daughters-in-Law	78
Questions for Daughters-in-Law	79
Chapter 8 – Courage to Compromise	80
Story 9	82
Discussion 9	84
Reflections for Daughters-in-Law	86
Questions for Daughters-in-Law	87
Chapter 9 – Tolerate Failures and Changes	88

Contents

Chapter 1 – Who's in Charge	11
Power Struggle	13
Decisions	14
Story 1	16
Discussion 1	19
Reflections for Daughters-in-Law	20
Questions for Daughters-in-Law	21
Chapter 2 – Triumph and Defeat	22
Story 2	26
Discussion 2	27
Reflections for Daughters-in-Law	29
Questions for Daughters-in-Law	30
Chapter 3 – Holiday Crisis	31
Story 3	32
Discussion 3	33
When Mothers-In-Law Visit	34
Gift Giving Nightmares	36
Reflections for Daughters-in-Law	38
Questions for Daughters-in-Law	39
Chapter 4 – Money Misery	40
Story 4	41
Discussion 4	43
Story 5	46
Discussion 5	47
Reflections for Daughters-in-Law	50
Questions for the Daughter-in-Law	51

DEDICATION

This book is dedicated with love
To my husband Paul J. Reynolds, who
Supported and encouraged me.

Copyright © 2017 Pamela Reynolds

All rights reserved.

Published by:
Blooming Twig Books
New York / Tulsa
www.bloomingtwig.co

ISBN-978-1-61343-122-1

The Princess and the Queen

A Guide for Daughters and Mothers-In-Law.

Drop the drama and live happily ever after.

Pamela Reynolds

Printed in the USA
CPSIA information can be obtained
at www.ICGtesting.com
LVHW021545270924
792324LV00010B/345